W9-DGS-969

Rock Gardens

DAVID SQUIRE

ROCK GARDENS

DAVID SQUIRE

Illustrated by Vana Haggerty

WHITECAP BOOKS

Designed and conceived by

THE BRIDGEWATER BOOK COMPANY LTD

Art Directed by PETER BRIDGEWATER

Designed by TERRY JEAVONS

Illustrated by VANA HAGGERTY FLS

Edited by MARGOT RICHARDSON

Managing Editor ANNA CLARKSON

CLB 3509

This edition published in 1995 by

WHITECAP BOOKS LTD

1086 West 3rd Street

North Vancouver

B.C.

Canada V7P 3J6

© 1995 CLB Publishing

Godalming, Surrey, U.K.

Printed and bound in Singapore

All rights reserved

ISBN 1-55110-242-0

CONTENTS

EARLY ROCK GARDENS

THE Japanese, more than a thousand years ago, used rocks as garden features, often combining them with water. Early European rock gardens – other than those formed of natural outcrops of rocks – appeared during the seventeenth century in mainland Europe; slightly later in Britain; and then as part of chinoiserie (Chinese fashion) gardens, a style introduced from France. The fashion of Chinese gardens also spread to North America, Germany, Sweden and Russia.

In the 1780s a rock garden was constructed by William Forsyth at the Chelsea Physic Garden, London, but is thought to have been mainly for scientific and geological interest, rather than as a botanical feature.

Grottos, which had been a feature of large gardens in Europe and Britain since the sixteenth century, were formed of rocks and often heavily decorated with shells, statues and illustrations.

THE SOOTHING, *slightly hypnotic sound of water was a major feature of this Irish rock garden in the 1800s.*

MOUNTAIN GREENERY

Few alpine plants have received such publicity as the European Edelweiss (Leontopodium alpinum), *a tufted herbaceous perennial, native to the Alps. It forms a clump of narrow, grey, basal leaves and flowers surrounded by white, woolly bracts. It is a curious and distinctive plant and suitable for rock gardens. However, it owes its fame less to the attractiveness of its flowers than to its 'press agent' Oscar Hammerstein II, lyricist and librettist of popular musicals, and of the famous 'Tyrolean' song.*

FORMAL *fountains and pools were often a part of rock gardens.*

LARGE *rock gardens in the early 1800s were often part of a natural outcrop of rocks. Bridges were frequently added as a novelty feature.*

ARCHES *of natural rocks would not be popular today, but in the early 1800s they were widely featured.*

FERNS AND EARLY PLANTS

Grottos were rich in ferns, which grow well in their damp, shaded conditions. Ferns were also a major plant in early rock gardens; it was not until the European custom – of growing alpine plants in pockets of soil between rocks – took hold that there was increased interest in rock gardens.

Integrating rock-garden plants with this type of gardening was demonstrated by several nurseries in the mid-1800s, although a few years earlier a style of creating imitations of specific mountain scenery had been initiated. This trend included replicas of the Matterhorn and Mount Fujiyama which were highly praised by gardening experts of the time.

POPULARIZING ALPINE PLANTS

During the early 1800s, discovering the flora of mountainous areas became increasingly popular and led to an interest in rock gardens. Brightly-flowered plants were discovered all over the world; in 1838 scarlet geraniums and rosette-forming violets were reported in the Bolivian Andes.

In the mid-1800s, the English nursery, Backhouse, did much to introduce and popularize rock-garden plants in Britain, while records indicate that many other nurseries were soon listing such plants in catalogues.

SAFEGUARDING ALPINES

There is always a temptation, when visiting mountainous areas, to pull up plants and to try to establish them in domestic gardens. They are relatively small plants and therefore easily smuggled home. But the result is the deprivation of natural flora on mountains. A wide range of plants is grown by many nurseries and if the ones you want are not readily available, specialist societies are able to put you in touch with suppliers.

ROCK GARDENS *and ponds were frequently combined, together with fountains and statues.*

ROCK GARDEN FEATURES

APART from natural slopes, there are many other places where rock-garden plants can be cultivated. Dry-stone walls create terraces on sloping land, while raised beds, with sides formed like dry-stone walls, enable plants to be grown at about waist height. They also introduce general height to gardens.

On patios, sink gardens make attractive features. Old stone sinks are traditional for this purpose, but white, glazed sinks can be modified and made equally attractive (see page 19).

Blocks of tufa can also make attractive features on patios and terraces, and are even sometimes used on balconies.

NATURAL *slopes create ideal situations for rock gardens. Rocks can be positioned to create natural strata (see page 12). Careful construction is essential, as once built it will be a major and permanent feature.*

FREE-STANDING *rock gardens make it possible to grow plants on flat sites. A pond adds further interest, and a small waterfall feature can also be added.*

DRY-STONE WALLS *are ideal homes for rock garden plants. Additionally, the walls can be used to create terraces (see page 15).*

RAISED BEDS *formed of attractive stones create features that make rock gardening possible in flat areas (see page 14). They also help to give height and variation to flat areas, as well as separating one part of a garden from another.*

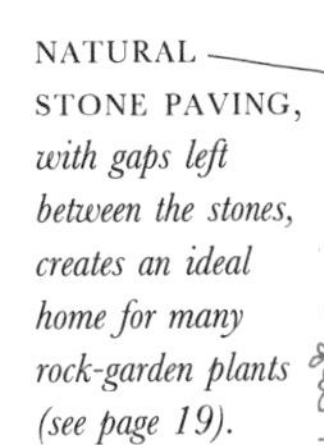
NATURAL STONE PAVING, *with gaps left between the stones, creates an ideal home for many rock-garden plants (see page 19).*

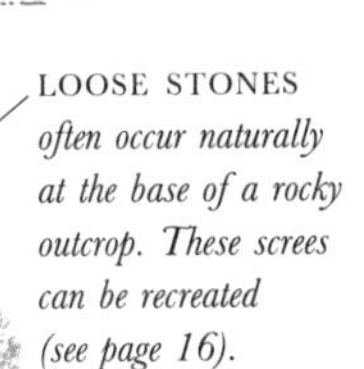
LOOSE STONES *often occur naturally at the base of a rocky outcrop. These screes can be recreated (see page 16).*

BLOCKS *of compressed peat form homes for acid-loving plants. These are ideal woodland features (see page 17). Peat beds are best formed on slight slopes so that the plants can be clearly seen.*

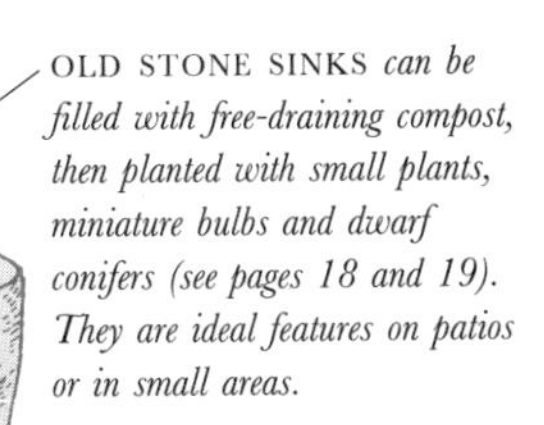
OLD STONE SINKS *can be filled with free-draining compost, then planted with small plants, miniature bulbs and dwarf conifers (see pages 18 and 19). They are ideal features on patios or in small areas.*

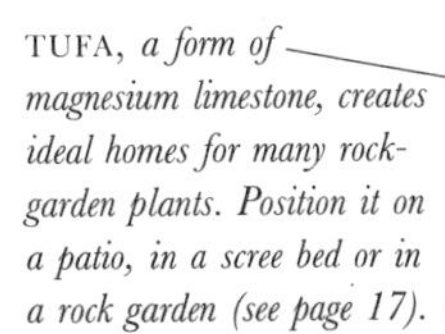
TUFA, *a form of magnesium limestone, creates ideal homes for many rock-garden plants. Position it on a patio, in a scree bed or in a rock garden (see page 17).*

SITE, ASPECT AND ROCKS

TO ENSURE the long-term success of a rock garden, it must be constructed with care and in a suitable position:

- Choose a site that faces the sun, although slight shade for part of the day is acceptable. Indeed, it is better to have light shade than to risk plants becoming over-heated, but it is most important to avoid constantly shaded positions.
- Do not position rock gardens under trees. They drip water on plants long after rain has stopped. Also, in autumn, leaves fall from deciduous trees and create constant dampness around plants, encouraging the presence of pests and onset of diseases.
- The soil must be well drained to prevent water remaining at the bases of stems and around roots during winter.
- A windbreak formed of evergreen conifers, on the side most exposed to cold winds, helps to protect plants during winter.
- Ensure that the area is free from pernicious perennial weeds such as Horsetail and Couch Grass. Once these weeds become established, it may be necessary to dismantle the whole rock garden and to sift all the soil.
- Check that soil pests such as wireworms and cockchafers are not present in great numbers. Newly dug pasture land is usually plagued with these pests.

EVERGREEN *conifers planted on the cold, windswept side will protect plants during winter. They help to filter strong wind and cause less turbulence than walls.*

CHOOSE *a bright, sunny position that is preferably lightly shaded during part of the day.*

CHOOSE *a place away from deciduous trees, which both shade plants and shed leaves in autumn.*

PREFERABLY, *the site should have a gentle slope which faces the sun.*

RANGE OF ROCKS

A wide range of stones can be used in rock gardens. Preferably use local materials, as they blend best with the surroundings. There are five main types of stone: sandstone, limestone, granite, slate and tufa (mentioned on page 17).

- *Sandstone: soft and mellow appearance, in several colours, has a coarse grain and weathering takes many years.*
- *Limestone: weathering is rapid and it soon loses its angular edges. However, it is not suitable for lime-hating plants.*
- *Granite: weathering is exceptionally slow; the stone is fine-grained and hard.*
- *Slate: weathering is not fast, but quicker than granite; available in shades of green, grey or purple. Initially, it has sharp edges.*

Granite

Westmorland

York Stone (sandstone)

Slate

Tufa

BUYING ROCKS

Choose the type of rock you want (see above), then contact a local supplier to enquire about its cost and the charge for haulage. The cost of carriage can be a major consideration, so telephone a few suppliers before making a decision.

Local stone will be cheaper and more likely to harmonize with its surroundings than stone quarried several hundred miles away. Do not mix different types and ensure it will be in a range of sizes.

Find out when the stone will be delivered and inspect it before it is unloaded. It should not be tipped from the delivery lorry, as this damages the surface of the stone.

There is always the temptation to pick up natural stones from the countryside and to take them home, but this is not only theft, it is also detrimental to the environment. In addition, it is never worth economizing by using broken pieces of concrete: these will be a permanent eye-sore, as the broken pieces do not have strata or a natural apearance. They will remain a heap of concrete, rather than a rock garden that will please.

MOVING *large stones can be a problem; large rollers and long crow-bars are one solution, or use a sack-trolley or wheelbarrow.*

AMOUNT OF STONE?

Estimates of the amount of stone required vary and, clearly, depend on the type of construction. Rock gardens with only a slight slope need fewer pieces of stone than a steep slope, or one where many layers (strata) are needed to keep the soil in place.

As an estimate of the amount of stone needed, a rock garden 3m/10ft square requires about 2 tonnes/4410lbs of stone, in a range of sizes.

ROCK GARDENS ON NATURAL SLOPES

A SLIGHTLY sloping area that faces the sun – but is lightly shaded for part of the day – provides the most easily constructed home for rock-garden plants. Unlike raised beds or free-standing rock gardens, little soil moving is needed, other than to ensure good drainage.

GOOD DRAINAGE

If the surface is slightly sandy and the top 30cm/12in of soil is exceptionally well drained, rocks can be laid directly on the surface. Usually, however, it is necessary to remove the top 25cm/10in of soil and to prepare the ground thoroughly. In the base, form a 10cm/4in-thick layer of clean bricks or stones. Ensure it is not contaminated with building rubbish. Firm this base and form a 5cm/2in layer of sharp sand on top. Rake this level and add about 10cm/4in of topsoil.

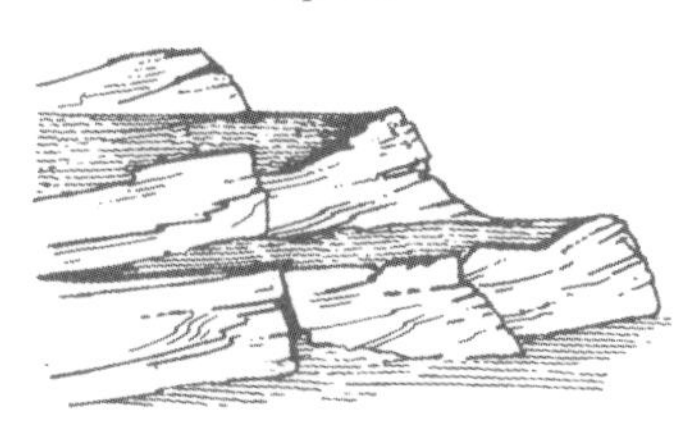

FORMING *a sloping terrace, with rocks appearing in natural-looking strata, is the normal way to construct a rock garden.*

SLOPING *outcrops, as they occur in nature, look good towards the base of rock gardens.*

LAYING THE STONES

Spread out the stones, so that their size, shape and strata can be seen. Start putting the stones in place from the base upwards. The two main formations for them are sloping, with the stones terraced and forming a natural stratum, or producing outcrops where the length of each stratum is limited and more at random.

Of these two, the terraced type is the easiest to create as the position of each stone is clearly dictated by its neighbour.

EARLY ROCK-GARDEN WRITERS

As nurseries started to grow, rock garden plants, gardening magazines and books featured them. Rock gardens were constructed at the Royal Botanic Gardens, Kew, in 1867 and four years later at the Royal Botanic Garden, Edinburgh. In 1870, the garden writer, William Robinson, published Alpine Flowers for English Gardens. *It was much acclaimed and an inspiration to rock-garden enthusiasts. Eight years later he included hardy-alpine and rock-garden plants in* Hardy Flowers, *while in* Gardening Illustrated *there were repeated suggestions to get rid of shells and other ornamentation and to focus on growing plants.*

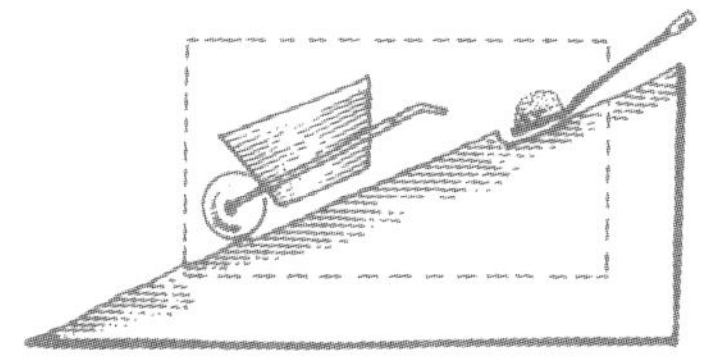

START *digging from the top of the slope, rather than the base. It is then easier to remove the soil.*

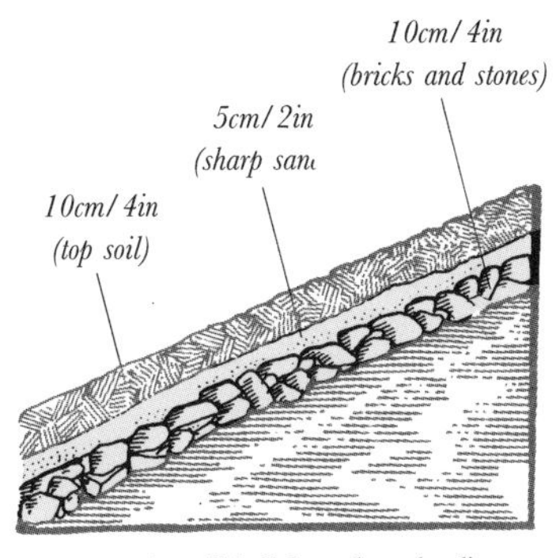

UNLESS *the soil is light and sandy, dig out the area to a depth of 25cm/10in.*

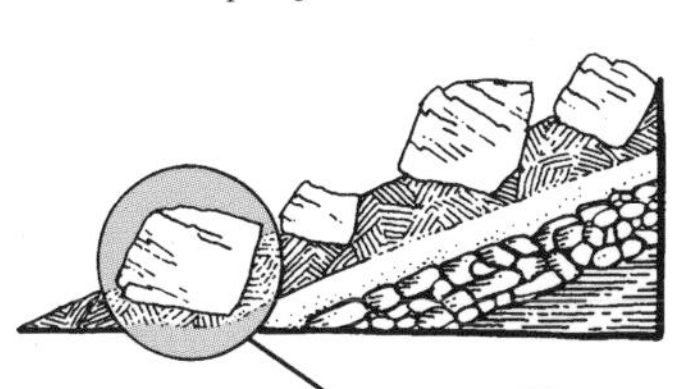

EACH STONE *must tilt backwards slightly, with one-third to one-half of it buried. This ensures it is firmly in the soil and appears natural. Never just spread the stones at random on the soil's surface; it disturbs the eye and does not look natural.*

PLANNING LARGE ROCK GARDENS

If the rock garden is large, it is possible to combine the 'sloping terrace' design with the 'outcrops'. At the base, use outcrops to give the impression that under the soil there are large rocks just peeping out. If space allows, form a pier of several rocks to create the impression of a continuous outcrop.

DESIGNING AND PLANNING

With large rock gardens the area must be planned on paper before setting rocks in position. Strings pegged on the soil's surface make it easy to judge how it will look and, if possible, arranging the stones on the ground in their approximate positions gives a fuller idea of the finished rock garden.

Getting extra large stones into position and manoeuvring them is a three-person job: two to move the stone and the other to view it from several paces away to gain an overall impression. A team is also necessary to reduce the risk of injury to backs and arms. As well, choose a day when the surface soil is dry: accidents are more likely to occur when both soil and rocks are wet; and the soil is soon turned to mud by repeatedly walking on it when wet.

LEAVE *small areas at the base of rocks so that plants can be put in them. Moisture runs off rocks and keeps roots moist and cool.*

RAISED BEDS

RAISED beds are ideal for introducing 'height' to flat gardens. They also create excellent homes for rock-garden plants. Because they are raised, they are easier for gardeners in wheelchairs, as well as those that cannot readily bend, to look after the plants. By restricting the bed's width to about 1.5m/5ft it is possible to reach most of the plants from a sitting position.

ECONOMIC CONSTRUCTION

Raised beds are cheaper to construct than rock gardens on slopes as the stones are cheaper; the sides can even be made from rail sleepers or re-constituted stone.

To ensure long life and safety, raised beds must be strongly constructed on sound foundations, especially if the walls are more than 30cm/12in high. Dig out a trench around the perimeter, fill with 5cm/2in of clean rubble, compact it and form 10cm/4in-thick concrete foundations. The lowest layer of bricks can then be cemented to the foundations, but leave weep-holes every 1.2m/4ft to enable surplus water to drain from the compost. The rest of the wall is formed by overlapping the bricks, and without the benefit of mortar. Do not construct the sides more than 90cm/3ft high.

FILLING THE CENTRE

When the walls are complete, fill the base one-third deep with clean rubble, then top up with friable, weed-free topsoil to within 2.5cm/1in of the top. Allow the soil to settle for a couple of weeks, then set the plants in position. After planting, form a layer of 2.5–3.6cm/1–1½in-thick stone chippings or 6mm/¼in shingle over the surface of the soil.

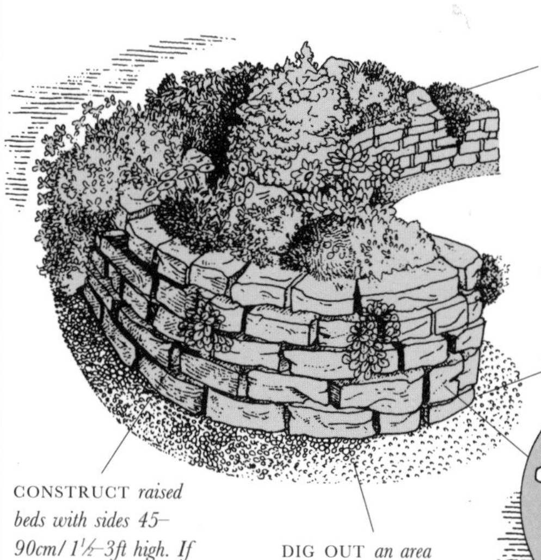

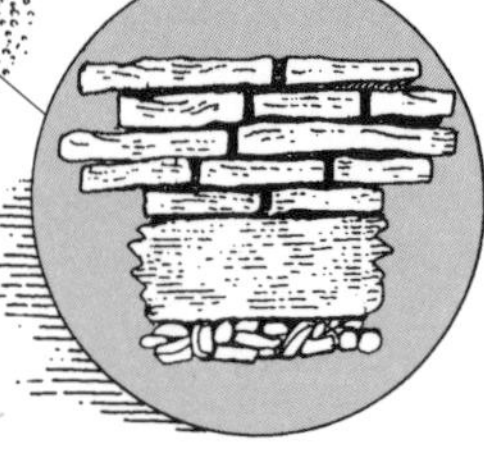

FILL *with well-drained friable topsoil to within 2.5cm/1in of the top of the wall.*

IF THE *wall is more than 30cm/12in high, form a strong base of compact rubble and 10cm/4in-thick concrete foundations.*

CONSTRUCT *raised beds with sides 45–90cm/1½–3ft high. If the sides are higher than 90cm/3ft, they may become unstable. The pressure of water tends to push out the sides.*

DIG OUT *an area 20–25cm/8–10in wide and 5–7.5cm/2–3in deep around the wall and fill with a 6mm/¼in layer of shingle.*

DRY-STONE WALLS

AS WELL as providing homes for rock-garden plants, dry-stone walls enable attractive terraces to be created. The height should be limited to 1.2m/4ft and weep-holes must be included every 1.2m/4ft along the base to enable surplus water to drain from the soil. If this is omitted, the pressure of water during wet winters will push over the wall. Battering the wall (leaning it backwards) and filling behind it with rubble also aids its long-term survival.

CREATING A STRONG BASE
Foundations are needed, similar to those necessary for raised beds. Cement the lowest two layers of stones together (allowing for seep-holes) and then continue upwards, fitting the stones together but not using mortar between them. Tilt each stone slightly backwards and set plants between them as each level is put in place. Pack soil firmly between the stones and around the plants. At the top, use slightly wider stones to form a capping. When it is complete, gently spray the wall with water until the plants are established.

When building a dry-stone wall, rather than just picking pieces of stone off a heap at random and trying to make them fit, it is easier to spread them out on the ground and to select those that naturally fit together.

SHINGLE EDGING

Along the wall's base, dig out a strip 5–7.5cm/2–3in deep and 20–25cm/8–10in wide. Fill it with 6mm/¼in shingle. This has several functions: it prevents grass growing close to the wall's base, enables trailing plants to bush out and trail to the wall's base without being damaged, and creates a distinct edging line for lawn mowers. In addition, it enables the lawn's edge to be cut with long-handled edging shears.

SCREE BEDS

SCREES naturally occur at the bases of cliffs or gullies and are formed of small, loose stones scattered on the surface. In gardens, it is possible to construct a scree bed at the lower end of a rock garden, creating further opportunities to grow rock garden plants. Screes are less expensive – and easier – to construct than rock gardens, and create large areas for plants.

Even if you do not have space for a rock garden, it is still possible to form a scree at the base of a wall, surrounded by a path to prevent surface stones being scattered.

> **ALPINE OR ROCK GARDEN PLANTS?**
>
> *The two terms are often used very loosely and have come to mean any plant which is suitable for growing in a rock garden. However, an alpine plant is one that lives on a mountain, above the upper limit of the tree line but below the area where snow lies throughout the year.*

CONSTRUCTING A SCREE

Mark out an area at the base of the rock garden; in nature, the area of a scree slowly widens, until from above it appears like a giant splash of water that has spread. Therefore, rather than tapering the scree to a point, gradually widen it to a mushroom-shape.

Dig out the area to 38cm/15in deep and fill the base with 15cm/6in of clean, compacted rubble. Form a 5cm/2in-thick layer of coarse sand or gravel over the rubble, then a mixture of one part topsoil, one of moist peat and three of grit. After plants have been put in place, form a 2.5cm/1in-thick layer of 6mm/¼in shingle over the surface. This coating ensures that the surface is well drained and that leaves do not rest on damp soil. It also prevents heavy drops of rain falling on soil and then splashing plants with dirty water.

It is not necessary to pack the area with plants, as the surface shingle looks attractive and forms a frame for the flowers and leaves.

TO CREATE *an impression that the scree bed is a natural feature, position a few large rocks to form a natural outcrop.*

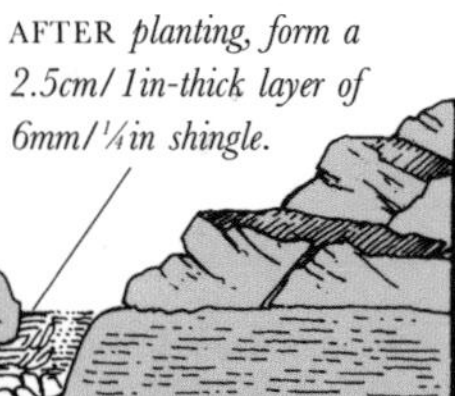

DIG SOIL *to 38cm/15in deep, form a compacted 15cm/6in-thick layer of clean rubble.*

FORM *a 5cm/2in layer of coarse sand or gravel over the rubble, them 15cm/6in of scree compost (see above).*

AFTER *planting, form a 2.5cm/1in-thick layer of 6mm/¼in shingle.*

PEAT BEDS

THESE are ideal places for growing acid-loving plants. They are not formed of stones and their similarity to rock gardens is the stratified layers of peat blocks which form and often enclose them. Occasionally, they are surrounded by logs or railway sleepers, especially when formed on a steep slope and where soil retention is vital.

Peat beds are best positioned in light shade, as most of the plants grown in them are native to woodland areas.

CONSTRUCTING PEAT BEDS
Before deciding to create a peat bed, check that the under-lying soil is not chalky. If it is, there is no point in forming the feature as even though the peat is initially acid, its continual absorption of chalky water will make it unsuitable for acid-loving plants. Use either a chemical-reaction pH kit, or one with a probe and a dial.

When on a flat surface or slight slope, the edging can be formed of peat blocks which have been soaked in water and allowed to drain slightly.

Use peat blocks to form levels in the same way as rocks in rock gardens. Fill with a mixture of equal parts peat and topsoil around and between the blocks of peat. After positioning the peat blocks and adding compost, allow them to settle for a couple of weeks before setting the plants in place. Last, cover the surface with moist peat or bark chippings.

TUFA GARDENS

Tufa is a type of magnesium limestone in which lime-hating plants can be grown. It is porous and absorbs and retains masses of water. Pieces of tufa are ideal for placing in rock gardens and scree beds, but it can also be featured on its own on patios: holes for plants can be chipped out with a hammer and chisel. When planting, wash most of the soil off the roots, push them into the hole and pack well-drained compost around them.

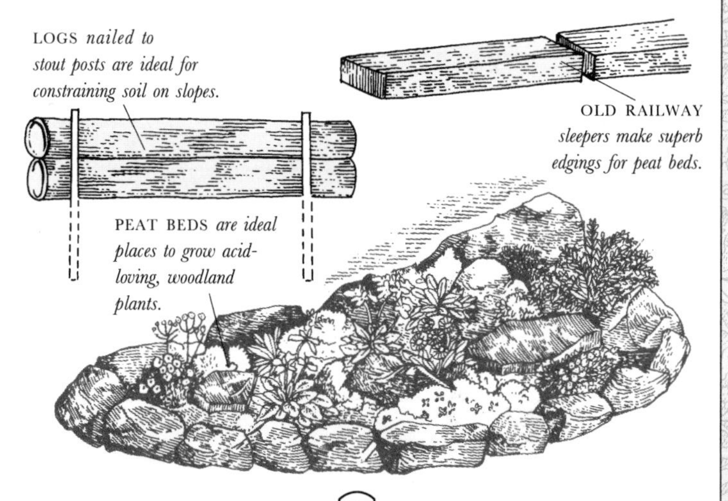

LOGS *nailed to stout posts are ideal for constraining soil on slopes.*

OLD RAILWAY *sleepers make superb edgings for peat beds.*

PEAT BEDS *are ideal places to grow acid-loving, woodland plants.*

SINK GARDENS

OLD stone sinks, with sides about 15cm/6in high, are ideal homes for small rock-garden plants. Miniature bulbs and dwarf conifers can be mixed with them, with trailing plants at the sides.

Old stone sinks are expensive, but an alternative is to modify a glazed sink (detailed on the opposite page). They are deeper than the earlier stone type and need more trailing plants to make the sides less bland.

Position on four strong bricks to prevent tilting.

PLANTING A STONE SINK

Thoroughly scrub the sink and position it on four strong house bricks. Do not place the sink directly on the ground as it is then too easy for slugs and snails to attack the plants. Make sure it does not tilt, but make it slope slightly towards the drainage hole.

Place a piece of perforated gauze over the plug hole and then put a layer of broken clay pots or pebbles over the base. Form a thin layer of sharp sand over this and half fill it with compost, made firm; use a mixture of equal parts topsoil (or potting compost), moist peat and grit. If lime-hating plants are being planted, ensure that the potting compost does not contain any chalk.

Place a couple of large rocks on the compost and adjust their height so that the stones are half buried. Add more compost, at the same time put in the plants. When planting is complete, the compost's surface should be about 2.5cm/1in below the rim. This allows for a 12mm/½in layer of

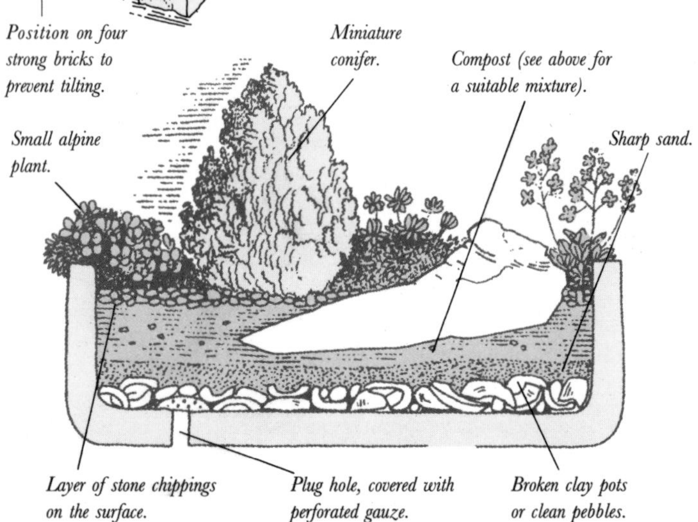

CONVERTING AN OLD GLAZED SINK

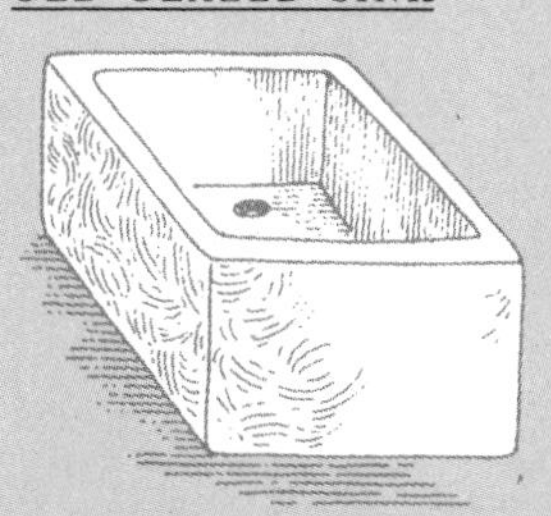

Thoroughly wash and remove grease from the inside and outside of the sink. Scratch the outside to roughen it, then coat with a PVA bonding glue. Mix equal parts of cement powder, sharp sand and peat, add water and coat the sides, top and about 5cm/2in down into the inside. Allow to dry for several weeks.

rock chippings or pea-shingle, and a 12mm/½in space between the rim and the shingle. This space at the top of the sink is essential to allow plants to be adequately watered and to prevent stone chippings falling out.

PLANTS TO CHOOSE

There are many small rock-garden plants to choose from and a wide range is featured throughout this book. But ones especially to look for include:

- *Androsace primuloides (A. sarmentosa):* Deep rose flowers during spring and early summer.
- *Antennaria dioica* 'Rosea': Deep pink flowers during late spring and early summer.
- *Campanula cochleariifolia:* Blue bells from mid-summer to autumn.
- *Edraianthus pumilio:* Lavender-blue flowers from late spring to mid-summer. Grey-green leaves.
- *Erinus alpinus:* Bright pink, starry flowers from early spring to late summer. Evergreen and tufted.
- *Hebe buchananii 'Minor':* White flowers during early summer.
- *Lewisia cotyledon:* Pink flowers with white veins during late spring and early summer.
- *Saxifraga burseriana:* Pure white flowers during late winter and early spring.
- Miniature bulbs such as *Narcissus cyclamineus, N. bulbocodium, Crocus chrysanthus, Iris danfordiae, I. reticulata, Eranthis hyemalis* and *Cyclamen coum.*

BETWEEN PAVING

Many small, low-growing rock-garden plants can be successfully grown in cracks between pieces of natural stone paving. These include species of thyme, arenaria, armeria, acaena, saxifraga and sedum. If the area is large, position the plants mainly at the edges, so that a clear path can be left where people mostly walk.

Plants growing in paving are especially at risk in winter.

- *Do not sprinkle salt over ice or snow to melt it, as it makes the soil toxic to plants. Also, do not scatter sand over the area as this damages the leaves.*

PLANTING AND LOOKING AFTER

THOROUGHLY inspect all plants before buying them and do not be tempted to buy a plant because it is cheap. If it dies soon after, it will have been an expensive mistake.

Most rock-garden plants are sold in spring. Inspect each one thoroughly: apart from the points detailed at the bottom of this page, check that the size of the plant is in balance with the pot. If the plant is much larger than the root area it indicates that it has been kept in the same pot for too long and that the roots are constricted. Conversely, if the soil-ball is much larger than the foliage it indicates that the plant has been re-potted recently and the roots may not be properly established.

LOOKING AFTER

Rock-garden plants are usually quite tough and hardy. Indeed, they readily withstand low temperatures, but, when combined with rain, this can be a lethal combination. For this reason, a mulch of pea-shingle helps to keep the leaves and stems dry.

WINTER PROTECTION

Plants with tender leaves may need protection from heavy rains during winter. Tents formed of small panes of glass can be propped up on bricks, but secure the glass so that it cannot be blown about and cause harm. The ends must be left open for ventilation. Small, tent-like cloches can also be used, but must be pegged into the soil to prevent them being blown about. Also, ensure they cannot harm children, cats and dogs.

Weeding, feeding, watering and mulching with shingle are the main jobs when looking after rock-garden plants. Every three or four years it may be necessary to lift plants in spring and to replant young pieces from around the outside of each clump.

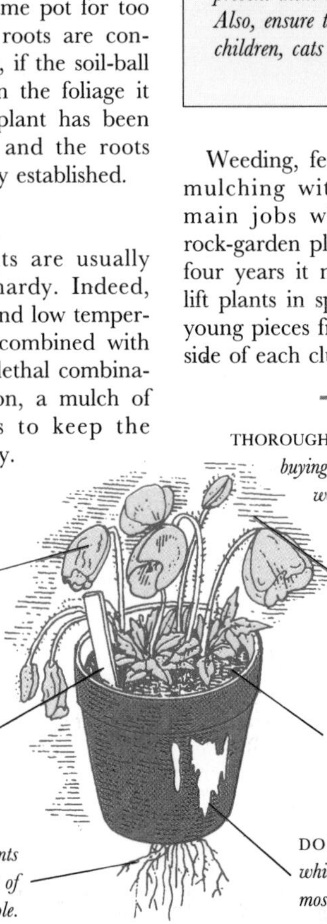

THOROUGHLY INSPECT *plants before buying them: look at the plant as well as the compost and pot.*

LEAVES *and flowers must not be damaged by pests and diseases.*

BRIGHT *young shoots indicate active growth.*

ENSURE *the plant is clearly labelled.*

COMPOST *should be moist but not waterlogged.*

DO NOT *buy plants with roots coming out of the drainage hole.*

DO NOT *buy plants which have slime or moss on the pot.*

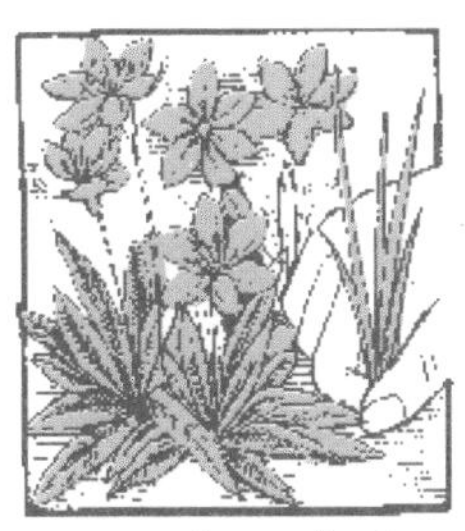

WEEDING *is a continual task, especially during spring and summer. Unfortunately, there is no alternative to removing weeds by hand; pull them up early, while they are still small.*

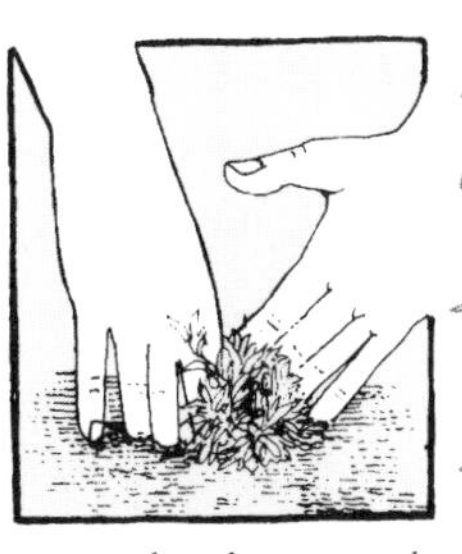

LIFT *and re-plant congested plants in spring. Carefully divide them and replant young pieces from around the outside of the clump. Discard the old, tough and woody parts at the centre.*

IN AUTUMN, *remove leaves that have blown on plants from nearby trees. If left, they cause dampness around plants and encourage decay and the presence of slugs and snails.*

FEED *plants in spring, if possible before topping up the mulch of stones around them. Choose a balanced feed, not one rich in nitrogen that subsequently causes too much lush growth.*

NEWLY PLANTED *young plants need frequent watering in spring and early summer until they are established. During prolonged dry periods watering is also necessary, but it must be thorough and not just dampen the soil's surface, which will do more harm than good. Do not moisten leaves or stems, as this causes decay.*

MULCHING *plants with an 18–25mm/¾–1in-thick layer of gravel chippings ensures leaves do not rest on soil. In addition, it prevents heavy splashes of rain falling on bare soil and then on plants. The chippings also act as a deterrent to snails and slugs. Instead of stone chippings, use bark chippings on peat beds.*

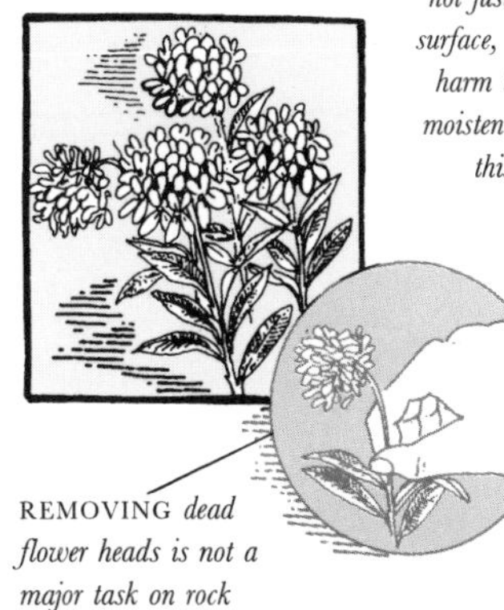

REMOVING *dead flower heads is not a major task on rock garden plants, but it does tidy them up.*

BY AUTUMN, *some plants may appear straggly and unkempt. This is the time to tidy them up and to remove long stems. If left, they encourage the presence of pests and the onset of decay. Do not leave this task until late winter or early spring, as newly emerging bulbs may be damaged, especially if you have to tread on the rock garden to reach some of the other plants.*

ROCK-GARDEN PLANTS

THE RANGE of plants grown in rock gardens is exceptionally wide, from true alpines to bulbs, dwarf conifers and shrubs. But the majority are perennials and popularly represented by Gold Dust *(Alyssum saxatile)*, aubretia, Rock Cress *(arabis)*, saponaria and saxifragas.

Rock-garden purists might blanch at the thought of such a medley of plants, but there are no set rules and only the imagination and enthusiasm of gardeners is the limiting factor.

SIZE LIMITATION

Although there is certainly an 'anything goes' philosophy about selecting plants, the size of the rock garden imparts its own limitations. The deciduous, purplish-red leaved and dome-shaped Japanese Maple *Acer palmatum* 'Dissectum Purpureum' and its green-leaved brother 'Dissectum', both grow up to 1.2m/4ft high and 1.8m/6ft wide. In a large rock garden they are superb, but for small areas they are too dominant. But there are many suitable dwarf shrubs – often prostrate and not more than 30cm/12in high – and these are ideal in even the smallest area.

MINIATURE BULBS

Few eyes are not captured by the flowers of bulbous plants in late winter and early spring. They are harbingers of a new season and once planted are easily grown. The initial cost of buying a few bulbs is more than repaid by their ability to produce flowers each year – and with no attention. They do, however, attract mice and often a layer of fine-mesh wire-netting, laid on the soil's surface, is needed to protect them in winter, when other food is scarce.

TRUE *alpine plants include Edelweiss* (Leontopodium alpinum) *and grow between the permanent snow line and the uppermost limit of trees. Edelweiss comes from the European Alps, while others originate in other mountainous areas.*

MINIATURE *bulbs, such as the Hoop Petticoat Daffodil* (Narcissus bulbocodium), *bring colour to rock gardens in late winter and early spring. Other bulbous or cormous types include crocuses, irises, scillas, tulips and cyclamen.*

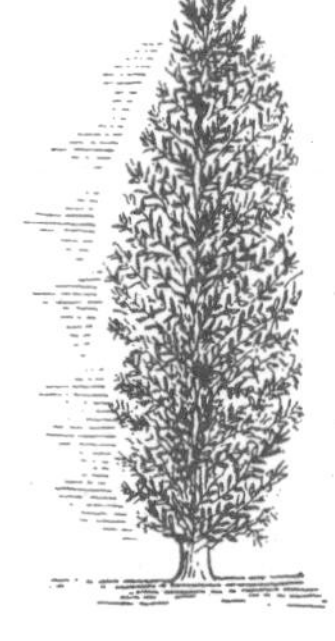

MINIATURE *and slow-growing conifers provide interest throughout the year. An example is* Juniperus communis *'Compressa', with greyish-green leaves and column-like stance. Other conifers are spreading, bun- or dome-shaped.*

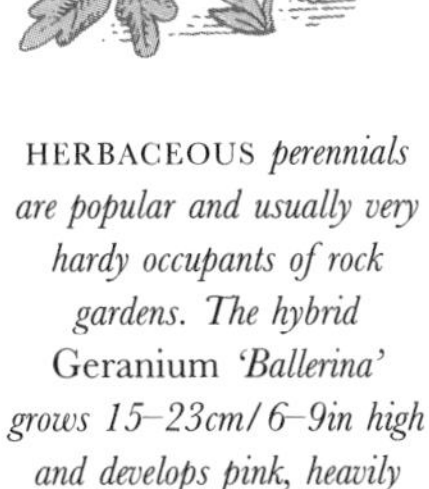

HERBACEOUS *perennials are popular and usually very hardy occupants of rock gardens. The hybrid* Geranium *'Ballerina' grows 15–23cm/6–9in high and develops pink, heavily veined flowers from early to late summer or early autumn.*

ANNUALS, *which are raised each year from seed, are superb 'fillers' for rock gardens. They are inexpensive and ideal for carpeting rock gardens in colour. Sweet Alyssum* (Lobularia maritima/Alyssum maritimum) *is an example.*

DWARF *shrubs create permanence in rock gardens and although some are large, others, such as the North American Sand Myrtle* (Leiophyllum buxifolium) *which forms an evergreen shrub about 30cm/12in high, are ideal.*

TEMPORARY COLOUR

During their early years, clothing the whole rock garden with permanent plants might be a financial problem and this is where annuals can help. Additionally, there are always bound to be gaps that need remedial attention in early summer.

Some annuals are hardy and can be sown where they are to flower; others need the comfort of gentle warmth in late winter or early spring to start them off. Annuals to consider include Sweet Alyssum (now properly called *Lobularia maritima* but more popularly and widely known by its early name *Alyssum maritimum*). Although hardy, it is usually raised as a half-hardy annual in gentle warmth. The Poached Egg Flower *(Limnanthes douglasii)* and Baby Blue Eyes *(Nemophila menziesii)*, however, can be sown where they are to flower.

There are also biennials to consider and these include Daisies *(Bellis perennis)* and the Alpine Wallflower *(Erysimum alpinum)*.

HARDY PERENNIALS *are the most widely grown occupants of rock gardens. These include* Arabis ferdinandi-coburgii *with white flowers and brightly variegated leaves. The form 'Variegata' has white-edged leaves.*

SUB-SHRUB

Some shrubs have a small nature, with a woody base and upper stems dying back each winter. In their own country they probably have a woody, permanent nature, but in cooler regions produce growth that does not survive during winter.

CORMS AND MINIATURE BULBS

Chionodoxa – Ipheion

MOST corms and bulbs planted in rock gardens flower during late winter and spring. Some, such as *Cyclamen coum,* flower in mid-winter, while *C. hederifolium (C. neapolitanum)* appear from late summer to early winter. Most have a miniature stance, about 15cm/6in or shorter, but a few are taller.

Spring-flowering bulbs and corms are planted in late summer or early autumn, as soon as they are available. Autumn and early winter-flowering types are planted in spring or early summer.

CORM OR BULB?

At first sight these appear quite similar and, indeed, they are both underground food storage organs that enable survival during periods when they are dormant.

- *Bulb: Formed of fleshy, modified leaves and with a bud-like structure. Within the centre of each bulb there is a dormant shoot.*
- *Corm: Formed of a swollen and thickened stem-base and covered with a papery skin. At the corm's top is a bud which produces a shoot and roots.*

IN GROUPS

These are diminutive and gregarious plants which look best when planted in small groups, where their colour impact is reinforced. When planting them, either take out a small, flat-based hole and spread out the bulbs to a few inches apart, and then return soil over them, or use a small trowel to plant them individually.

Early spring bulbs such as crocuses, chionodoxas and irises benefit from being planted in the shelter of a large rock, whereas autumn and early winter-flowering types are better in large displays.

With all of these bulbs, avoid spreading them too thinly and over a large area, as their impact will be lost. Always mark the area they occupy to avoid other plants being inadvertently planted on top, or too close to them.

Never plant bulbs in soil that is badly drained, as they will decay. Preferably, choose well-drained but moisture-retentive soil. Add peat if the soil is light and sandy, but mix in sharp sand where slight drainage is needed. If the area is boggy, installation of drains is essential.

CHIONODOXA LUCILIAE *(Glory of the Snow) grows 15cm/6in high and during late winter and early spring creates a wealth of light blue, white-centred flowers. Plant them 7.5cm/3in apart.*

CROCUS CHRYSANTHUS, *7.5–10cm/3–4in high, has golden-yellow flowers during late winter and early spring. There are also white, blue and purple types. Plant them 7.5cm/3in apart.*

CYCLAMEN COUM *grows about 7.5cm/ 3in high and develops 18mm/ ¾in-long flowers in shades of pink and carmine from mid-winter to early spring. These appear above kidney-shaped, mid-green, marbled leaves. Plant them 10cm/ 4in apart.*

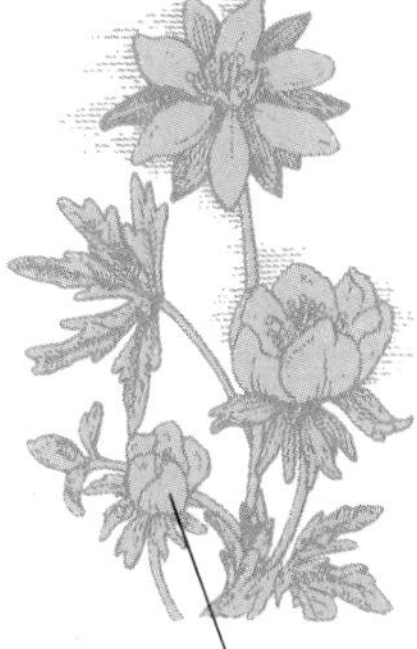

FRITILLARIA PALLIDIFLORA *is up to 30cm/ 12in high and therefore is best suited to large rock gardens. During mid-spring, clusters of yellow, bell-shaped flowers appear with grey-green leaves. Plant 15cm/ 6in apart.*

ERANTHIS HYEMALIS *(Winter Aconite) has lemon-yellow, cup-shaped flowers, 2.5cm/ 1in wide and backed by a light-green ruff, during late winter and spring. These are 10cm/ 4in high and borne amid deeply cut leaves. Plant the bulbs about 7.5cm/ 3in apart.*

CYCLAMEN HEDERIFOLIUM, *the Baby Cyclamen, earlier called* Cyclamen neapolitanum, *grows 10cm/ 4in high and develops mauve to pink flowers from late summer to early winter. Plant them 13cm/ 5in apart.*

IPHEION UNIFLORUM *(Spring Starflower) forms clumps with white to violet-blue flowers, about 15–20cm/ 6–8in high, during mid and late spring. The flowers are slightly scented. Plant the bulbs about 7.5cm/ 3in apart.*

FRITILLARIA MELEAGRIS *(Snake's Head Fritillaria/ Checkered Lily), 30–38cm/ 12–15in high, bears bell-shaped, 36mm/ 1½in long, white and purple checkered flowers during mid and late spring. The flowers seldom fail to attract attention. Plant them about 13cm/ 5in apart.*

NATURAL DIE DOWN

After the flowers fade, allow them to die down naturally. Also, do not disturb the leaves while they wilt, shrivel and die. If they are tied up, the food value in them does not return to the bulb; pulling off leaves is even worse. When all signs of life have left them, the remnants of loose leaves can be gently pulled up, but without disturbing the bulbs or corms.

CORMS AND MINIATURE BULBS
Iris – Tulipa

ROCK-garden corms and bulbs are superb on their own but can be further enhanced by combining them with other plants. Here are a few combinations to consider:

- *Chionodoxa luciliae* (Glory of the Snow) has blue flowers during late winter and early spring. Plant Gold Dust *(Alyssum saxatile)* so that its golden-yellow flowers highlight those of the bulb.
- *Cyclamen coum* and the Winter Aconite *(Eranthis hyemalis)* form a pleasing partnership, flowering in mid-winter and early spring.
- The Winter Aconite is also a superb partner for clumps of Snowdrops, such as *Galanthus nivalis* 'Flore-pleno'.
- For a medley of shape and colour use the yellow-flowered *Narcissus cyclamineus* 'February Gold' with the blue-headed *Chionodoxa luciliae.* This combination of plants flower in late winter and early spring.
- *Scilla tubergeniana* and the Winter Aconite form a pleasing colour and shape combination.

ANGEL'S TEARS

The Spanish native Narcissus triandrus *'Albus' has dropping, creamy-white flowers during early and mid-spring. It is known as Angel's Tears and several stories exist about the way this name was gained. They differ slightly but all revolve around the distress or euphoria of a Spanish guide called Angelo or Angel. One story tells of him making an exhausting climb and breaking into tears when finding this plant.*

IRIS DANFORDIAE *has a diminutive stance, only 10cm/ 4in high. During mid and late winter it produces sweet and honey-scented, vivid lemon flowers about 7.5cm/ 3in across. Plant the individual bulbs 7.5–10cm/ 3–4in apart.*

IRIS DOUGLASIANA *is a tall, Californian species, 30–45cm/ 12–18in high. Each stem bears up to five 7.5cm/ 3in-wide flowers in shades of lavender and bluish-purple in early summer. Plant the bulbs 38–45cm/ 15–18in apart.*

IRIS INNOMINATA *is another North American iris, about 15cm/ 6in high and bearing buff, cream, yellow or orange flowers about 6.5cm/ 2½in wide during early summer. It is ideal for planting in peat beds. Plant it 23cm/ 9in apart.*

- *Tulipa tarda*, with its early and mid-spring flowers can be combined with the Pasque Flower *(Pulsatilla vulgaris)*.
- Form a spring-flowering combination of *Tulipa kaufmanniana* 'The First' and the perennial-type *Potentilla tabernaemontani*, also known as *R. verna* and the Spring Cinquefoil. It has bright yellow flowers about 12mm/½in wide from mid to late spring.
- For an unusual combination try *Iris reticulata* and wild thyme.

IRIS RETICULATA *is popular, 15cm/6in high and widely grown. During late winter and early spring it develops deep bluish-purple flowers with orange blazes. Plant the bulbs 7.5–10cm/3–4in apart.*

NARCISSUS BULBOCODIUM *(Hoop Petticoat Daffodil) is 7.5–13cm/3–5in high and bears yellow, hoop-like trumpets during late winter and early spring. Plant them about 7.5cm/3in apart.*

NARCISSUS CYCLAMINEUS *has petals that sweep back, away from the trumpet. They grow 15–20cm/6–8in high and flower in late winter and early spring. Plant them 7.5cm/3in apart.*

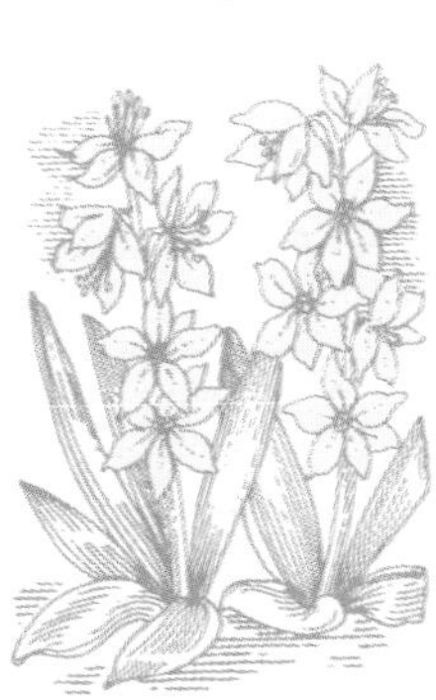

SCILLA TUBERGENIANA, *one of the squills, grows 7.5–10cm/3–4in high and has pale blue flowers in late winter and early spring. Plant it with the Common Snowdrop* (Galanthus nivalis). *Plant the bulbs 7.5–10cm/3–4in apart.*

TULIPA KAUFMANNIANA *(Waterlily Tulip) grows 15–25cm/6–10in high, with star-like flowers during early and mid-spring. The normal species is white with red and yellow flushes. Plant the bulbs about 13–15cm/5–6in apart.*

TULIPA TARDA *is popular, 15cm/6in high and several flowers are borne in terminal clusters on each stem during early and into mid-spring. They are white, with a large, bright centre. Plant the bulbs 3.5–10cm/3–4in apart.*

MINIATURE AND SLOW-GROWING CONIFERS

Chamaecyparis – Juniperus

CONIFERS introduce permanency to rock gardens. They also create features around which other plants can be clustered for protection. Miniature conifers usually remain relatively small, but slow-growing types are planted while small and although they grow slowly there comes a time when they are too large. At this stage, dig them up in spring and plant into a large tub or garden.

Renew the soil where the conifer was growing and replant another, preferably in spring. After planting – and especially if the weather is warm – keep the soil moist and lightly mist-spray the foliage several times a day.

CHAMAECYPARIS LAWSONIANA *'Aurea Densa' is compact and slow growing, with densely packed, flattened sprays of golden-yellow leaves. Initially it is bun-shaped; about 50cm/20in high after ten years.*

CHAMAECYPARIS LAWSONIANA *'Ellwood's Pillar' has a miniature habit, reaching only 50–60cm/20–24in after ten years. The beautiful foliage is compact, bluish-grey and feathery. It is especially attractive in winter.*

CHAMAECYPARIS LAWSONIANA *'Pygmaea Argentea' is slow growing and rounded, with bluish-green foliage tipped creamy-white. Even after ten years it is seldom more than 45cm/18in high.*

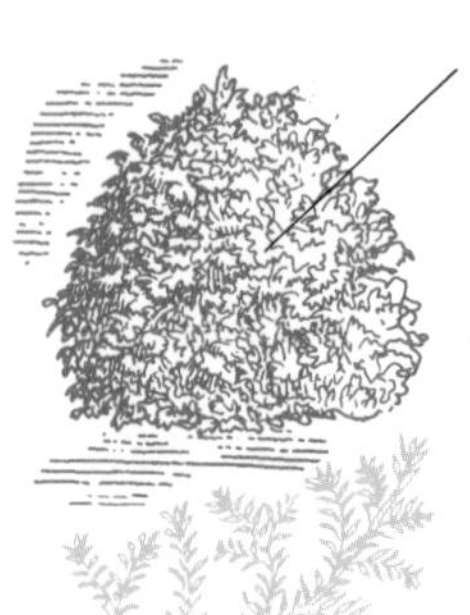

CHAMAECYPARIS PISIFERA *'Squarrosa Sulphurea' has a rounded shape and its juvenile foliage is a bright sulphur colour. After ten years it is about 75cm/2½ft high.*

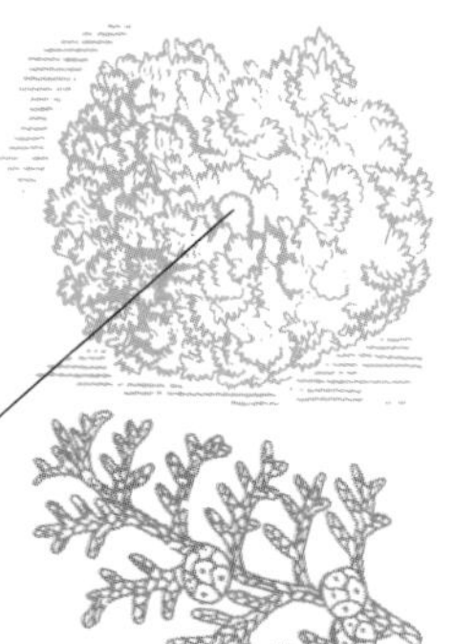

CHAMAECYPARIS OBTUSA *'Nana Lutea' is superb in winter, with bright yellow foliage. After ten years it is only 50–60cm/20–24in high.*

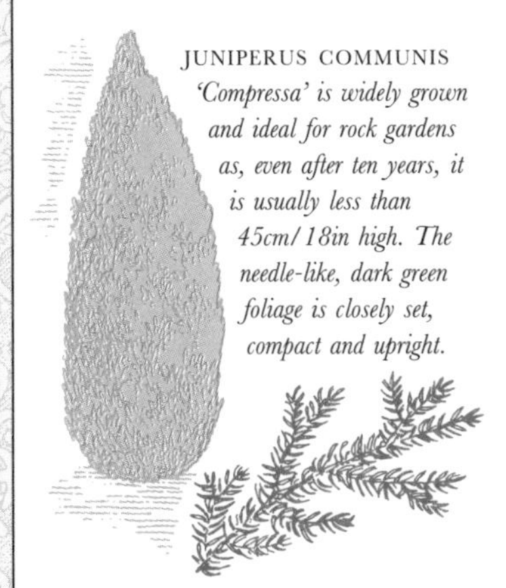

JUNIPERUS COMMUNIS *'Compressa' is widely grown and ideal for rock gardens as, even after ten years, it is usually less than 45cm/18in high. The needle-like, dark green foliage is closely set, compact and upright.*

JUNIPERUS COMMUNIS *'Depressa Aurea' is prostrate, with golden-yellow foliage in spring, turning bronze in winter. After ten years it is about 30cm/12in high and 1.2m/4ft wide.*

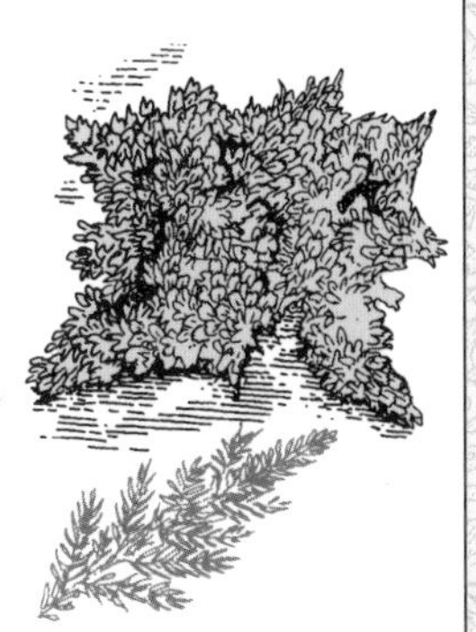

JUNIPERUS COMMUNIS *'Golden Showers' reveals yellowish-bronze foliage in winter and bright yellow in spring as growth commences. After ten years it reaches 1.2–1.5m/4–5ft high. Reserve it for large areas.*

JUNIPERUS *X* MEDIA *'Gold Sovereign' is a superb conifer with a low, spreading nature, and bright yellow foliage throughout the year. After ten years it is about 50cm/20in high and 75cm/2½ft wide.*

JUNIPERUS SQUAMATA *'Blue Star' has a bushy, somewhat sprawling nature with steel-blue, needle-like foliage. After ten years it is about 38cm/15in high and 45cm/18in wide, and creates a superb feature.*

PLANTING INTO A GARDEN

Large conifers removed from rock gardens are more difficult to move and establish than small ones. This is because the roots have a larger area of foliage to supply with moisture. If, after moving a conifer in spring, the weather becomes cold and windy, either insert a stake as a temporary support, or use guy-ropes. Also, by reducing the flow of cold air over the foliage the strain on the roots to absorb moisture is reduced. Either form a screen of hessian supported by stakes, or put a layer of straw or hay between two layers of wire-netting and support it on the windward side of the conifer. If the weather is dry, water the soil regularly and also mist-spray the foliage.

When transferring a miniature conifer – especially a tall one – from a rock garden into a pot, place it initially in a wind-sheltered corner until it is established and self-supporting.

MINIATURE AND SLOW-GROWING CONIFERS

Juniperus – Thuya

All conifers in rock gardens need careful positioning, especially as they form a permanent framework. Some conifers are tall, others bun-shaped or even prostrate, and they all need careful consideration before selecting their positions. When too large they can, of course, be moved to a container or part of a garden (see page 29), but this should not be done regularly.

LARGE ROCK GARDENS

In a large rock garden there is more opportunity to use tall and dominating conifers, perhaps with a few narrowly columnar types such as *Taxus baccata* 'Standishii' or the pencil-thin *Juniperus virginiana* 'Skyrocket'. If there is a path that meanders through a large rock garden, these conifers can be positioned on either side of it. However, do not plant narrow and tall conifers at the very top, as they will look like chimney pots. Instead, put them at the base, or half to three-quarters of the height up the mound so that from a distance they fuse and harmonize the rock garden with the background and sky.

BUN-SHAPED

Small, bun-shaped miniature conifers are easier to position, but more attention needs to be given to their colour. Bright yellow, grey, as well as steel-blue ones are available; the yellow and golden ones immediately capture the eye and can be too dominant at the front of a rock garden. Steel-blue and blue-grey conifers are especially attractive in winter when surrounded by snow. Therefore plant them on flat areas and where they can be readily seen when surrounded with snow.

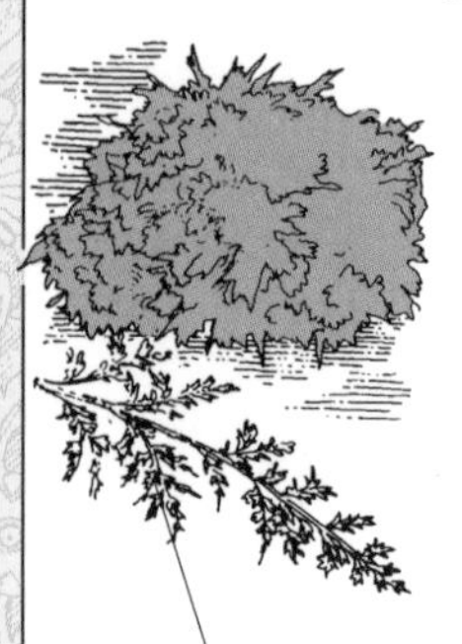

JUNIPERUS SQUAMATA *'Holger' has a spreading habit and eventually is suitable only for large rock gardens when, after ten years, it is about 50cm/20in high and 75cm/2½ft wide. In spring it is creamy yellow, but is bluish-green in winter.*

JUNIPERUS VIRGINIANA *'Skyrocket', also sold as* J. scopulorum *'Skyrocket', has a pencil-thin outline and greyish-blue foliage. After about ten years it will grow to 1.8m/6ft high.*

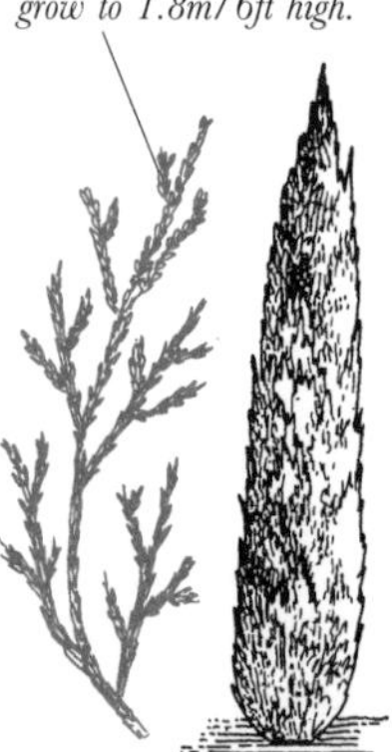

PINUS SYLVESTRIS *'Beauvronensis' is a dwarf form of the Scots Pine, reaching only 60cm/2ft high and 3m/3½ft wide in ten years. The foliage is grey-green and forms a beautiful feature, especially in spring with its new growth.*

TAXUS BACCATA *'Standishii' is slow growing and creates a narrow column of gold leaves. In ten years it is about 1m/ 3½ft high and may need to be moved. Nevertheless, it is well worth planting at the base of a rock garden.*

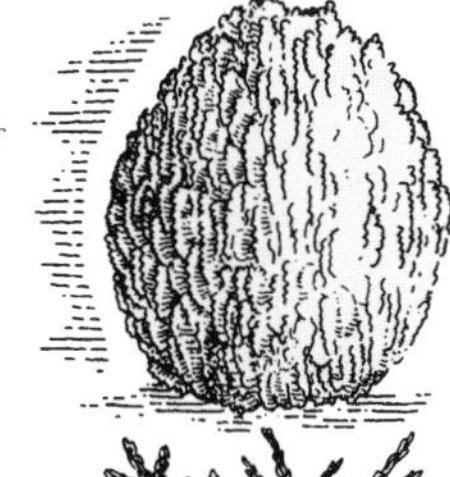

THUYA PLICATA *'Stoneham Gold' has bright, rich golden-yellow foliage during summer as well as in winter. After ten years it is usually between 60cm/ 2ft and 90cm/ 3ft high. If a beacon of colour is needed, choose this conifer.*

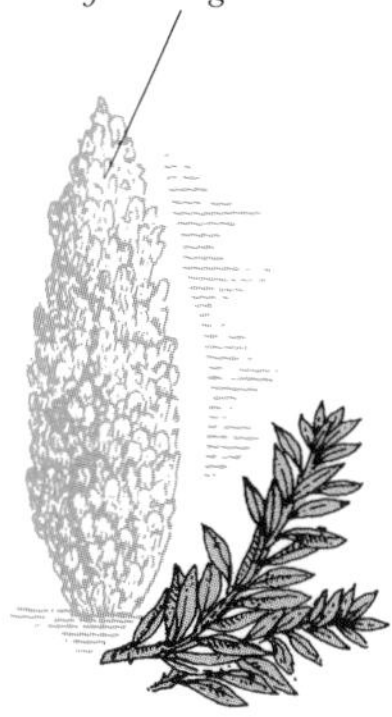

THUJA ORIENTALIS *'Aurea Nana' forms a rounded cone-shape, packed with vertical fans of yellow-green foliage. In winter it becomes tarnished gold. After about ten years this conifer is often still only 60cm/ 2ft high.*

FURTHER DWARF CONIFERS

All measurements given here are after ten years of growth.
- Chamaecyparis lawsoniana *'Ellwood's Gold': Soft, feathery, gold-tinged foliage in summer (1.2m/ 4ft high).*
- Chamaecyparis lawsoniana *'Gnome': Miniature stature, with deep green foliage (20–30cm/ 10–12in high).*
- Chamaecyparis lawsoniana *'Minima Aurea': Yellow leaves (50cm/ 20in high).*
- Chamaecyparis lawsoniana *'Minima Glauca': Globular (60cm/ 2ft high).*
- Chamaecyparis obtusa *'Nana Gracilis': Sprays of dark green foliage (60cm/ 2ft high).*
- Chamaecyparis pisifera *'Boulevard': Intense silver-blue foliage (90cm/ 3ft high).*
- Picea abies *'Little Gem': Dwarf, with bright new shoots in spring (30cm/ 12in high).*

Prostrate types need to be seen from above and from relatively close-by; therefore, use them by the sides of paths and towards the front of a rock garden.

SCREE BEDS

Although dwarf conifers are not traditionally part of scree beds, they nevertheless look handsome there and can be used instead of rocks to create height. Grey or steel-blue conifers look best. Choose three bun-shaped species and use them to indicate decreasing height. Always use odd-numbered plants in this situation. They create height contrasts and form attractive backgrounds for small groups of miniature bulbs. And, by using conifers that are blue-leaved, white and yellow flowers are especially highlighted.

Towards the lower edge of a scree bed, perhaps where it meets a path or lawn, plant a prostrate miniature conifer so that its foliage cuts across both features. If possible, position it so that the foliage spreads downwards, not up.

DWARF SHRUBS AND TREES
Acer – Euryops

THERE is a surprisingly wide range of dwarf shrubs and trees suitable for planting in rock gardens. Some are best reserved for large areas, but there are many that grow only 15cm/6in high so they can be fitted into small places.

In addition to the shrubs and small trees illustrated and described on these and the following two pages, there are others to consider, including:

- *Cotoneaster congestus* 'Nanus' is dwarf and evergreen, less than 30cm/12in high and with bluish-green leaves and red berries.
- *Cotoneaster dammeri* is 5–7.5cm/2–3in high and with a wide spread, often to 1.8m/6ft. It is therefore only suitable for large rock gardens. The evergreen leaves are dark green and glossy, with white flowers in early summer and round, red berries in late summer and autumn.

CALLUNA VULGARIS *(Heather/Ling) is a hardy evergreen with varieties in many colours and sizes, from 10cm/4in to 60cm/2ft. Select small varieties.*

COTONEASTER MICROPHYLLUS THYMIFOLIUS, *a mound-forming and prostrate evergreen shrub about 30cm/12in high and 50cm/20in wide, has white flowers and red berries.*

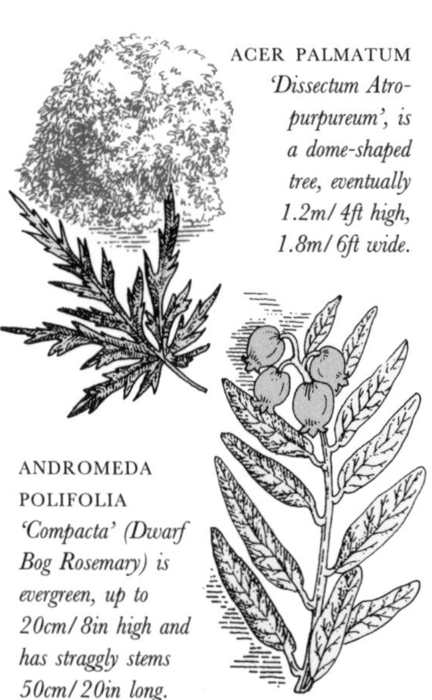

ACER PALMATUM *'Dissectum Atropurpureum', is a dome-shaped tree, eventually 1.2m/4ft high, 1.8m/6ft wide.*

ANDROMEDA POLIFOLIA *'Compacta' (Dwarf Bog Rosemary) is evergreen, up to 20cm/8in high and has straggly stems 50cm/20in long.*

- *Cytisus ardoini* is 20cm/8in high with an arching habit and golden-yellow flowers which appear during mid and late spring.
- *Cytisus demissus* is seldom more than 10cm/4in high, with large yellow flowers during late spring.
- *Cytisus decumbens* is prostrate, about 15cm/6in high and with bright yellow flowers during late spring and early summer.
- *Erica herbacea* (earlier known as *E. carnea*) has several low-growing varieties, some 15cm/6in high.
- *Erica cinerea* 'Coccinea', a form of Bell Heather, is 15cm/6in high and bears deep carmine-red flowers from early summer to autumn. There are several other low-growing varieties.
- *Erica tetralix*, the Cross-leaved Heath, has grey foliage and pink flowers throughout summer.

• *Genista lydia* is only suitable for large rock gardens; its stems, up to 60cm/2ft high, are covered with golden-yellow flowers during late spring and early summer.
• *Genista sagittalis* has winged, prostrate stems and bright yellow flowers during early summer.
• *Thymus drucei* (Wild Thyme and earlier known as *T. serpyllum*) grows up to 7.5cm/3in high and 60cm/2ft wide, with flowers in a range of colours from white, through pink to red, from early to late summer. 'Annie Hall' is smaller, with pale pink flowers, while 'Coccineus' is rich crimson.
• *Vaccinium vitis-idaea* (Cowberry/Mountain Cranberry) is evergreen, semi-prostrate and up to 15cm/6in high with a 45cm/18in spread. It is ideal for planting in peat beds, where it develops white or pale flowers during late spring and early summer.

DAPHNE ARBUSCULA, *a rounded and dwarf, evergreen shrub with fragrant, rosy-pink flowers from mid-spring to early summer, is about 15cm/6in high. It also develops brownish-yellow berries.*

EURYOPS ACRAEUS, *a dwarf evergreen shrub, grows about 30cm/12in high and slightly wider. During late spring and early summer, the silver-grey leaves are surrounded by bright yellow, 2.5cm/1in-wide daisy-like flowers.*

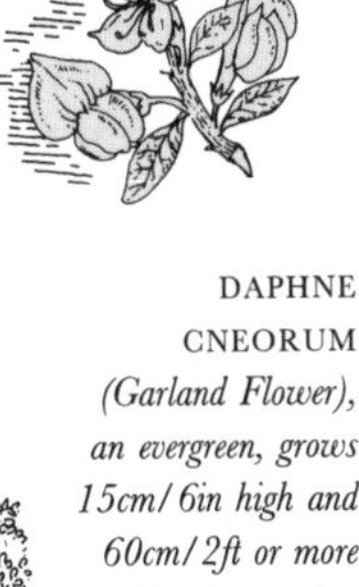

CYTISUS *X* BEANII, *a deciduous shrub 45–60cm/1½–2ft high, is suitable only for large rock gardens. It has golden-yellow flowers during late spring and early summer. It should be positioned where the stems can cascade.*

DAPHNE CNEORUM *(Garland Flower), an evergreen, grows 15cm/6in high and 60cm/2ft or more wide. During late spring and early summer it has scented, rosy-pink flowers. There is also a white form, 'Pygmaea', which is prostrate.*

DYERS' WEED

Genistas are superbly bright garden plants. Earlier, Genista tinctoria *was known as the Dyer's Greenweed or Dyer's Broom. It yields a strong yellow dye and from early times was used to dye wool. When combined with Woad it created a green dye known as Kendal Green. Kendal Green was the name of the place where the process was first introduced by Flemish immigrants during the eighteenth century.*

The plant is European, and grows up to 90cm/3ft high and 1.8m/6ft wide. From early to late summer it bears deep yellow flowers. The form 'Humifusa' is prostrate, up to 10cm/4in high and 60cm/2ft wide.

DWARF SHRUBS AND TREES
Genista – Zauschneria

SOME dwarf shrubs and trees are fully hardy and able to withstand the coldest of climates. Others, such as the Californian Fuchsia *(Zauschneria californica)*, are not always able to survive the rigours of winter in temperate climates, except when planted in warm positions. Light and dry soil also helps in their survival.

LOW-GROWING SHRUBS
Many of these plants are naturally low to enable survival in cold and exposed areas, where strong winds would batter and destroy tall, upright types. In addition, they are mainly deciduous, so that a fresh cloak of new, undamaged leaves appears each year. And being low, they are often covered by a protective layer of snow during winter. *Salix arbuscula*, for example, is native to Scandinavia, Northern Russia and Scotland, all areas where strong winds soon damage tall and exposed shrubs.

ACID-LOVING SHRUBS
Many shrubs must be given acid conditions, such as those present in peat beds. If planted into chalky soil they soon die. Suitable plants include some of those featured on these and the previous pages, such as:

- *Andromeda polifolia* 'Compacta'
- *Leiophyllum buxifolium*
- *Pimelea coarctica*
- *Polygala chamaebuxus*
- *Salix arbuscula*
- *Vaccinium vitis-idaea*

Other acid-loving shrubs include:

- *Gaultheria miqueliana:* Evergreen, up to 30cm/12in high and with dark green leaves. Bears small white flowers in early summer and white berries in autumn.
- *Galtheria procumbens* (Partridge Berry/Winter Green/Checkerberry): A North American evergreen up to 15cm/6in high and spreading to 90cm/3ft or more. Masses of shiny, dark green leaves and white or pink flowers in mid and late summer. Red berries.

GENISTA PILOSA *forms a neat shrub up to 45cm/18in high and spreading to 90cm/3ft. It drenches the ground with whip-like shoots and small, yellow flowers from late spring to mid-summer.*

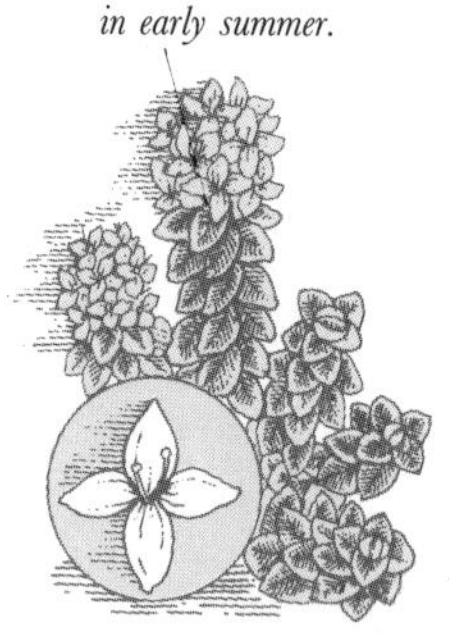

HEBE BUCHANANII *'Minor' is only 5cm/2in high and 10–15cm/4–6in wide, and ideal for planting in a sink garden. Its dull green, evergreen leaves form an attractive foil for the small, white, stemless flowers in early summer.*

HEBE VERNICOSA *forms an evergreen shrub about 20cm/8in high. The reddish-brown stems bear thick, fleshy, mid-green leaves tipped pale yellow. White, 2.5cm/1in-wide flowers appear in mid-summer.*

• *Vaccinium nummalaria:* Evergreen and compact, with arching shoots clothed in small, dark, glossy-green leaves. It grows about 25cm/10in high and during late spring and early summer bears rosy-red flowers, followed by black, round, edible berries.

• *Vaccinium praestans:* A creeping deciduous shrub, up to 10cm/4in high, with bell-shaped, white to reddish flowers in early summer. These are followed by 12mm/½ in-wide bright, glossy red berries. In North America it is known as Kamchatka Bilberry.

HYPERICUM OLYMPICUM *'Citrinum' is evergreen, with large, lemon-yellow flowers during mid and late summer. It grows about 25cm/10in high and 30cm/12in wide. The ordinary type has golden-yellow flowers.*

PIMELEA COARCTICA *(also sold as* P. prostrata*) is evergreen, with grey-green leaves, occasionally edged red, and white flowers in early summer. This plant has an attractive prostrate nature and spreads up to 60cm/2ft.*

LEIOPHYLLUM BUXIFOLIUM *forms an evergreen shrub that requires an acid soil, such as in a peat bed. It grows about 30cm/12in high and during early summer bears clusters of starry, white flowers which are at first pink.*

POLYGALA CHAMAEBUXUS *(Ground Box), is a dwarf, evergreen shrublet 10–15cm/4–6in high. From late spring to mid-summer it bears cream and yellow flowers tipped with purple. It must be planted in acid soil.*

ZAUSCHNERIA CALIFORNICA *(Californian Fuchsia) is distinctive, with red, tubular, fuchsia-like flowers during late summer and autumn. It grows up to 45cm/18in high and is not fully hardy in cold, exposed and wet areas.*

SALIX ARBUSCULA *(Dwarf Willow) is a low-growing, deciduous shrub with creeping woody stems, up to 45cm/18in high and spreading to 60cm/2ft. The leaves are deep green, and slender, grey catkins appear in mid-spring.*

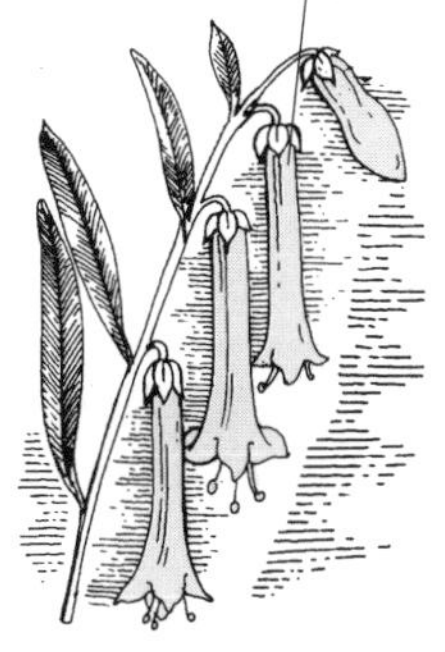

ANNUALS AND BIENNIALS

Adonis – Felicia

THESE are popular and inexpensive flowers, easily raised from seeds and certain to brighten rock gardens from late spring to the frosts of autumn.

• Half-hardy annuals: These are sown in seed-trays in late winter or early spring in a greenhouse and given gentle warmth until they germinate. The temperature is then reduced slightly and when the seedlings are large enough to handle they are transferred to other seed-trays and spaced out, so that each plant has more space. Later they are progressively acclimatized to outdoor conditions and planted out when all risk of frost has passed.

• Hardy annuals: These are sown in mid to late spring in the positions in which they are to flower. Sow seeds thinly and when the seedlings are large enough to handle, thin them out, usually to between 15cm/6in and 30cm/ 12in apart, depending on the species. The seed packet will indicate the distance.

• Biennials: These are sown one year to produce flowers during the following one. Sow seeds in a seed-bed outdoors, in a sheltered position, during late spring and early summer. When the seedlings are large enough to handle, thin them to between 5cm/ 2in and 10cm/4in apart, depending on the species, but ensure they are not left congested throughout summer. Keep the seed-bed regularly watered and free from weeds. In early autumn, transfer plants to their flowering positions. In exceptionally cold areas, moving them can be delayed until early spring.

ANAGALIS ARVENSIS *'Caerulea' (form of the Scarlet Pimpernel): Hardy annual; 5cm/ 2in high; thin to 15cm/ 6in apart. Dark blue, saucer-shaped flowers during summer.*

ANTIRRHINUM MAJUS *(Snapdragon): Half-hardy annual; choose low-growing varieties; plant 20–25cm/ 8–10in apart. It acts as a perennial in mild areas and will grow again the following year.*

ADONIS AESTIVALIS *(Pheasant's Eye): Hardy annual; 30cm/ 12in high; thin to 30cm/ 12in apart. Deep crimson, cup-shaped flowers in summer. Light green leaves.*

ALYSSUM MARITIMUM *(now correctly* Lobularia maritima *and widely known as Sweet Alyssum): Half-hardy annual; 7.5–15cm/ 3–6in high; plant them 20cm/ 8in apart. Flowers throughout summer.*

CALANDRINA UMBELLATUM *(Rock Purslane): Perennial usually grown as a half-hardy annual or biennial; 15cm/ 6in high; plant 23cm/ 9in apart. Magenta flowers, from mid-summer to autumn.*

ASPERULA ORIENTALIS *(Annual Woodruff): Hardy annual; 30cm/ 12in high; thin to 10cm/ 4in apart. Mid-green leaves and blue flowers.*

LOOKING AFTER BIENNIALS

These are hardy plants that are able to survive outdoors during winter. However, when young they are equally as susceptible to slug damage as other plants.

In spring, re-firm soil around the roots of biennials planted in autumn; frost often loosens the soil and if not firmed the plants do not grow rapidly. In autumn, when transplanting them, put a few plants to one side to act as spares for plants that do not survive the winter.

ERYSIMUM ALPINUM *(Alpine Wallflower/ Fairy Wallflower): Biennial; 20cm/ 8in high; plant them 10–15cm/ 4–6in apart. Bushy, with dark green leaves and scented, sulphur yellow flowers during late spring and early summer.*

LOOKING AFTER ANNUALS

Once they are planted, half-hardy annuals need little attention, except to keep them free from weeds, and to water the soil regularly during dry periods. Once these plants suffer from dry soil, they mature rapidly and do not fully recover, whatever treatment then given.

Hardy annuals are better equipped to withstand dry periods, but even these suffer and may not recover. When the seedlings are 7.5–10cm/3–4in high, insert pea-sticks between and around them so that stems and leaves grow up and through them. If the pea-sticks later appear to be too high, use secateurs to cut them off so that only leaves and flowers can be seen.

Check the plants regularly to ensure pests are not present, and spray as necessary. Slugs and snails are the biggest problem when plants are young.

ESCHSCHOLZIA CALIFORNICA *(Californian Poppy): Hardy annual; 30-38cm/ 12-15in high; thin them 23cm/ 9in apart. Blue-green leaves and bright-faced, poppy-like flowers.*

FELICIA BERGERIANA *(Kingfisher Daisy): Half-hardy annual; 15cm/ 6in high; plant 15cm/ 6in apart. Daisy-like, light-blue flowers from early summer to autumn. It creates a magnificent display.*

ANNUALS AND BIENNIALS
Ionopsidium – Portulaca

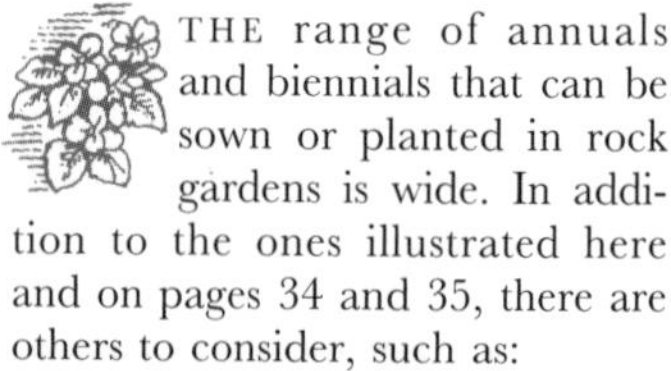

THE range of annuals and biennials that can be sown or planted in rock gardens is wide. In addition to the ones illustrated here and on pages 34 and 35, there are others to consider, such as:

• *Anagalis linifolia* 'Gentian Blue' is grown as a half-hardy annual, reaches 15–23cm/6–9in high and bears blue flowers from early to late summer. Plant it 25–30cm/10–12in apart.

• *Eschscholzia caespitosa* (also known as *E. tenuifolia*) is a hardy annual, and grows 13cm/5in high. From early summer to autumn it has blue-green, finely divided leaves and 2.5cm/1in-wide yellow flowers. Thin the seedlings to 15cm/6in apart.

• *Felicia bergeriana* (Kingfisher Daisy) is a half-hardy annual, 15cm/6in high and bearing steel-blue flowers with yellow centres from early to late summer. Space the plants about 15cm/6in apart.

• *Gazania* x *hybrida*, usually raised as a half-hardy annual, grows 23cm/9in high and from mid-summer to the frosts of autumn has a wealth of large, daisy-like flowers in many colours. Space 25–30cm/10–12in apart.

• *Gilea lutea* (Stardust and earlier known as *Leptosiphon hybridus*), a hardy annual, grows 10–15cm/4–6in high and from early summer to autumn has a feast of brightly-coloured, star-shaped flowers. Mixed-coloured varieties include flowers in yellow, orange, red and pink. Thin the seedlings to 10cm/4in apart.

• *Linaria maroccana* (Toadflax) is a hardy annual that grows 20–30cm/8–12in high and during early and mid-summer creates a wealth of snapdragon-like flowers in colours including violet, blue,

IONOPSIDIUM ACAULE *(Violet Cress): Hardy annual; 7.5cm/3in high; not necessary to thin them. Small, four-petalled, pale mauve or white flowers tinged with purple from early summer to autumn.*

LIMNANTHES DOUGLASII *(Poached Egg Flower): Hardy annual; 15cm/6in high; thin to 10cm/4in apart. Light green leaves and yellow, saucer-shaped flowers edged in white from early to late summer.*

LINUM GRANDIFLORUM 'RUBRUM' *(Scarlet Flax): Hardy annual; 30cm/12in high; thin to 13cm/5in apart. Easily grown annual, well known for its saucer-shaped, bright-crimson flowers and pale green leaves.*

NEMESIA STRUMOSA: *Half-hardy annual; 20-45cm/ 8-18in high; plant them 10-15cm/ 4-6in apart. Yellow, orange, pink, scarlet, cherry-red and blue flowers from early to late summer.*

NEMOPHILA MENZIESII *(Baby Blue Eyes): Hardy annual; 23cm/ 9in high; thin them 15cm/ 6in apart. White-centred, sky-blue, saucer-shaped flowers from early to late summer.*

NIEREMBERGIA *'Mont Blanc': Half-hardy annual; 15cm/ 6in high; plant 15cm/ 6in apart. Compact and spreading, with masses of 2.5cm/ 1in-wide white flowers throughout summer.*

red, yellow and pink. They are borne amid narrow, light green leaves. Thin the seedlings to 15cm/6in apart.

• *Mesembryanthemum criniflorum* (Livingstone Daisy), grown as a half-hardy annual, is 10–15cm/ 4–6in high and displays daisy-like, pink, crimson, orange, rose and apricot flowers from early to late summer. Space these succulent plants about 30cm/12in apart.

PORTULACA GRANDIFLORA *(Sun Plant): Half-hardy annual; 15-23cm/ 6-9in high; plant them 15cm/ 6in apart. Bright-green leaves and saucer-shaped, red, purple or yellow flowers with bright-yellow centres from early summer to autumn.*

• *Phacelia campanularia* is a hardy annual with grey leaves and blue, bell-shaped flowers about 2.5cm/1in wide from early summer to the frosts of autumn. Thin the seedlings to 15cm/6in apart.

• *Platystemon californicus* (Cream Cups) is a hardy annual, about 30cm/12in high and superb when grown in drifts in large rock gardens. During mid-summer it has masses of saucer-shaped, 2.5cm/ 1in-wide, pale yellow or cream flowers. Thin the seedlings to 10cm/4in apart.

• *Ursinia anethoides* is a half-hardy annual, growing 23cm/9in high and bearing orange, daisy-like flowers with purple centres from early to late summer. Space the plants 25cm/10in apart.

• *Verbena* x *hybrida* is grown as a half-hardy annual and creates a wealth of colourful flower heads in a range of colours from early summer to autumn. For growing in rock gardens, choose dwarf varieties, about 23cm/9in high, and plant them 15–23cm/6–9in apart.

ROCK GARDEN PERENNIALS

Acaena – Arabis

THESE are plants that, once planted, continue for several years before having to be lifted, divided and young pieces from around the outside replanted.

The range of perennials is wide and they are featured from this page to pages 56 and 57. They are always popular and form the main range of plants grown in rock gardens, filling them with both beautiful, colourful flowers and attractive leaves

- *Acaena buchananii* (New Zealand Burr), grows 2.5–5cm/1–2in high and spreads to 60cm/2ft, has grey-green leaves and amber-brown burrs.
- *Achillea tomentosa*, growing 15–20cm/6–8in high and spreading to 30cm/12in, develops downy, grey-green leaves. Bright yellow flowers, in heads up to 7.5cm/3in across, appear from mid-summer to autumn.
- *Aethionema* 'Warley Rose', 10–15cm/4–6in high and spreading to 38cm/15in, is ideal for rock gardens and dry-stone walls. Its leaves are grey-green, with rosy-red flowers in dense heads during spring and early summer.

LIVE-FOR-EVER

During the late sixteenth century, the herbalist and barber-surgeon John Gerard wrote that Antennaria dioica *was widely known as Live-long and Live-for-ever. He referred to brown-yellow thrumme (thread-like material) collected from the centre of flowers and which could be kept for a long time. For this reason, the plant was also known as both Life Everlasting and Mountain Everlasting.*

ACAENA MICROPHYLLA *(New Zealand Burr) grows up to 5cm/2in high and spreads 45cm/18in or more. When young the leaves are silvery, later bronze-green. The characteristic crimson burrs appear from mid-summer onwards and form an attractive display.*

AETHIONEMA PULCHELLUM *grows 15–23cm/6–9in high and about 38cm/15in wide. It forms mats of leaves and from late spring to mid-summer bears heads of pale pink, cross-shaped flowers. It needs well-drained soil.*

ALYSSUM SAXATILE *(Gold Dust) grows 15–30cm/6–12in high and spreads to 45cm/18in, with an evergreen, shrubby nature. From mid-spring to early summer it bears golden-yellow flowers. There are several varieties.*

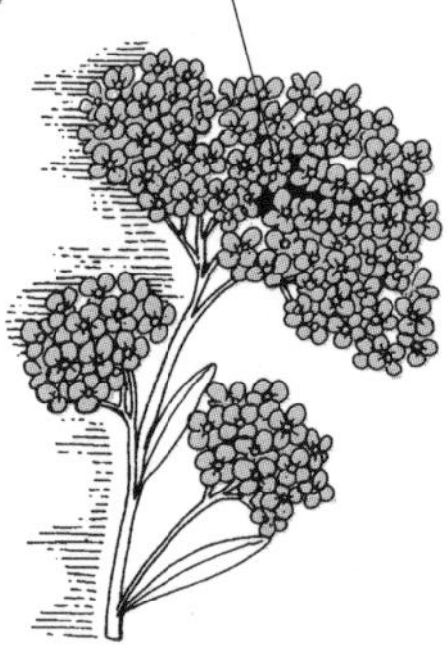

• *Alchemilla alpina* (Alpine Lady's Mantle), 15cm/6in high and about 25cm/10in wide, has silvery-edged green leaves and star-shaped, yellowish-green flowers from early to late summer. Often used in flower arrangements.

• *Androsace lanuginosa* (Rock Jasmine), 36mm/1½in high and spreading to 38cm/15in, forms trailing mats of silver-green leaves, with pink flowers from early summer to autumn. 'Leichtlinii' has white flowers with a red centre.

ANACYCLUS DEPRESSUS *(Mount Atlas Daisy) grows about 5cm/2in high and spreads to 30cm/12in. The finely divided, grey-green leaves are smothered with 5cm/2in-wide, white flowers from early to late summer. Remove dead ones regularly.*

ANDROSACE PRIMULOIDES *'Chumbyi' (Rock Jasmine and sometimes sold as* A. sarmentosa *'Chumbyi') is 10cm/4in high and spreads to about 45cm/1½ft. From mid-spring to early summer it bears headsof rose-pink flowers.*

ANDROSACE SARMENTOSA *(Rock Jasmine) grows 10–13cm/4–5in high and spreads to 60cm/2ft. From mid-spring to early summer it displays dome-shaped heads of rose-pink flowers on 5–10cm/2–4in-long stems.*

ANTENNARIA DIOICA *'Rosea' (Cat's Ear/Rosy Pussy Paws) is 10–15cm/4–6in high and spreads to 45cm/1½ft, with deep pink flowers borne amid a creeping mat of stems during late spring and early summer. Well-drained soil is essential.*

AQUILEGIA FLABELLATA PUMILA *(Alpine Columbine) grows 10–15cm/4–6in high and wide, with nodding, cap-like, pinkish-mauve flowers from late spring to mid-summer. The flowers appear above beautiful bluish-green leaves.*

ARABIS CAUCASICA *(Rock Cress and earlier known as* A. albida*) is 23cm/9in high and spreads to 50cm/20in or more. From early spring to early summer it displays white flowers above grey-green and hoary leaves. Cut it back as soon as the flowers fade.*

ROCK-GARDEN PERENNIALS

Arabis – Aubrieta

In addition to the rock garden perennials illustrated here, there are other superb plants to choose from.

- *Arenaria grandiflora* grows 5–7.5cm/2–3in high and spreads to 25cm/10in. It has bright green leaves and displays white, funnel-shaped flowers from late spring to late summer.
- *Arenaria montana*, 10–15cm/4–6in high and spreading to 45cm/18in, forms a mat of mid-green leaves. During late spring and early summer the leaves are smothered in bright white, saucer-shaped flowers.
- *Arenaria purpurascens*, 7.5cm/3in high and spreading to 30cm/12in, develops purple, star-shaped flowers during mid and late summer.
- *Armeria maritima* (Common Thrift), 15–23cm/6–9in high and spreading to 30cm/12in, is more vigorous than *A. caespitosa* (illustrated). In large rock gardens, however, it grows in dominant grey-

LADIES' CUSHION

*This is another of the many common names given to Thrift (*Armeria maritima*), together with Sea Pink and Gilly Flower. At one time, it was botanically known as* Statice maritima *and* S. armeria, *and was introduced into Tudor gardens when knot gardens became fashionable. The English gardener and herbalist, John Parkinson, in the early seventeenth century wrote of Thrift being one of the first plants used for forming knot gardens. It was clipped into shape. The Romans knew of this plant's ability to reduce sand erosion, while medicinally it was credited with 'stopping the Humours'.*

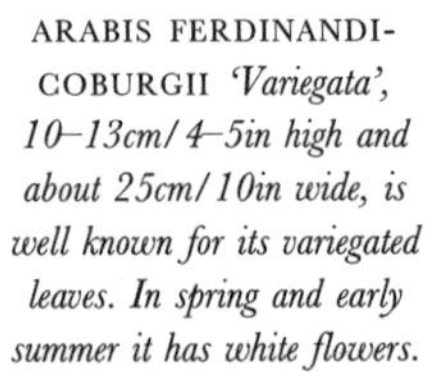

ARABIS FERDINANDI-COBURGII *'Variegata', 10–13cm/4–5in high and about 25cm/10in wide, is well known for its variegated leaves. In spring and early summer it has white flowers.*

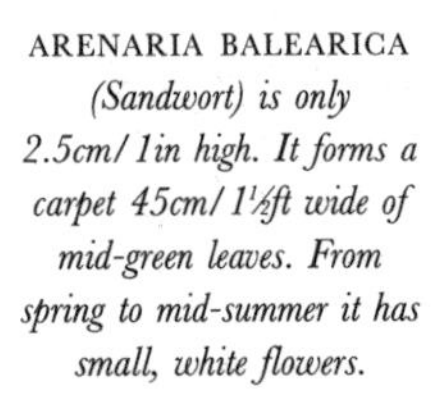

ARENARIA BALEARICA *(Sandwort) is only 2.5cm/1in high. It forms a carpet 45cm/1½ft wide of mid-green leaves. From spring to mid-summer it has small, white flowers.*

ARMERIA CAESPITOSA *(Thrift), 5–7.5cm/2–3in high, forms a 15–23cm/6–9in-wide, evergreen mound of grey-green leaves. During late spring it develops pink flowers.*

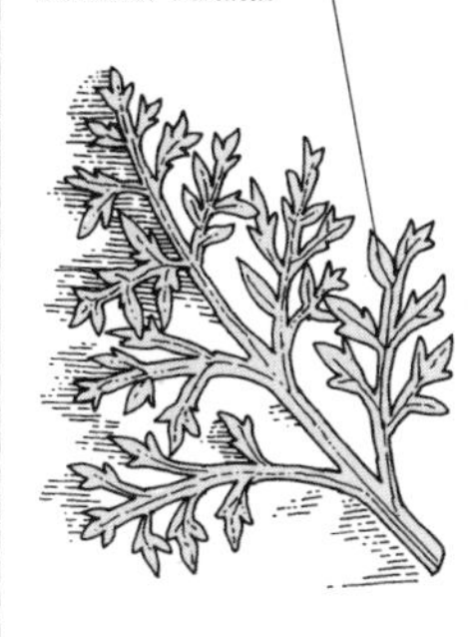

ARTEMISIA SCHMIDTIANA *'Nana' is dwarf, only 7.5cm/3in high and 30cm/12in wide. In autumn, the finely divided silvery-grey leaves form an attractive mound.*

ASPERULA SUBEROSA, *an alpine species, is only 7.5cm/3in high and spreads to 15cm/6in. It develops shell-pink flowers in early and mid-summer. In winter, protect it from rain.*

ASTER ALPINUS *is only 15cm/6in high and clump forming. During mid-summer it has purple-blue, 25–36mm/1–1½in-wide, daisy-like flowers with orange-yellow centres.*

green hummocks peppered from late spring to mid-summer with pink flower-heads up to 2.5cm/1in wide. There is also a white-flowered form.

• *Artemisia nitida* (also known as *A. lanata*), up to 5cm/2in high and spreading to 23cm/9in, forms grey-green, evergreen cushions. The leaves are finely dissected and yellow flowers appear from mid-summer to early autumn.

• *Asperula lilaciflora caespitosa*, up to 7.5cm/3in high and spreading to 15cm/6in, has bright green leaves and lilac-pink, tubular flowers during early and mid-summer.

• *Astilbe glaberrima saxatalis*, 10–15cm/4–6in high and wide, has finely dissected leaves and pale pink and cream flowers from early to late summer. Position astilbes towards the base of a rock garden, where the soil is moist.

ASTILBE CHINENSIS *'Pumila' is a diminutive rock-garden astilbe, about 23cm/9in high and 30cm/12in wide. From mid-summer to autumn it has rose-purple flower spires.*

AUBRIETIA DELTOIDEA, *7.5–10cm/3–4in high and spreading to 60cm/2ft, is smothered in purple to rose-lilac flowers during spring and early summer. There are many varieties.*

AUBRIETIA DELTOIDEA *'Aureovariegata' is about 7.5cm/3in high and spreads to 45cm/1½ft. The leaves are handsomely variegated in green and gold, and it has lavender flowers.*

ROCK-GARDEN PERENNIALS

Campanula – Edraianthus

CAMPANULAS are popular and easily grown rock garden perennials and in addition to the two illustrated here there are others that are well worth growing.

• *Campanula carpatica*, 23cm/9in high and spreading to 38cm/15in, is best in large rock gardens. During mid and late summer it bears cup-shaped flowers in colours ranging from blue to purple. There is also a pretty white-flowered variety.

• *Campanula portenschlagiana* (also known as *C. murialis*), 15cm/6in high and spreading to 45cm/18in or more, is long-lived and with heart-shaped, mid-green leaves. From early summer to late autumn it bears purple, bell-like flowers. It can be rampant, so be prepared to cut it back when the flowers fade.

• *Campanula zoysii*, 7.5cm/3in high and spreading to 15cm/6in, is sufficiently diminutive for most rock gardens, although it tends to be short-lived. Preferably, it needs the comfort of an alpine house, but will survive outdoors when given protection from excessive moisture during winter. Its light blue flowers appear during mid-summer.

CAMPANULA GARGANICA, *at 13–15cm/5–6in high and spreading to 30cm/12in, has mid-green, kidney-shaped leaves and massed blue flowers from late spring to autumn.*

DIANTHUS

Pinks offer an amazing range of plants for rock gardens. The Cheddar Pink (*Dianthus gratianopolitanus*) is illustrated here, but there are others worth considering, many of which are superbly scented.

CAMPANULA COCHLEARIIFOLIA (C. pusilla *and widely known as Fairy Thimbles) is 10–15cm/4–6in high and spreads to 30cm/12in. Blue, bell-shaped flowers.*

CERASTIUM TOMENTOSUM *(Snow-in-Summer) is 10–15cm/4–6in high and spreads to 45cm/1½ft. The leaves are woolly and oblong and from late spring to mid-summer covered with white flowers.*

CASSIOPE LYCOPODIOIDES *is mat-forming and often classified as a shrub. It is 5–7.5cm/2–3in high and spreads to 38cm/15in. White flowers appear in mid and late spring.*

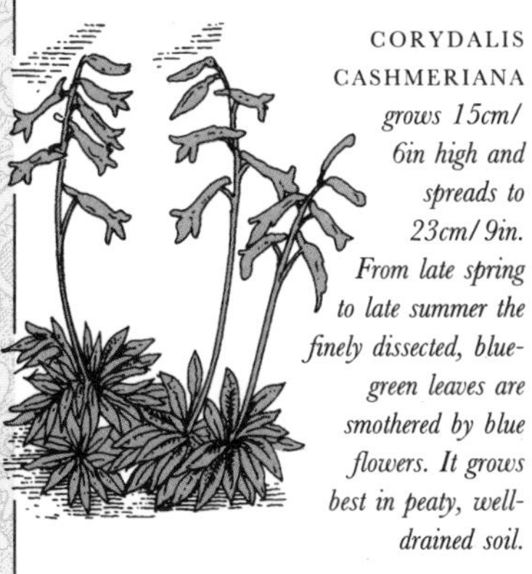

CORYDALIS CASHMERIANA *grows 15cm/6in high and spreads to 23cm/9in. From late spring to late summer the finely dissected, blue-green leaves are smothered by blue flowers. It grows best in peaty, well-drained soil.*

DIANTHUS GRATIANOPOLITANUS *(Cheddar Pink and earlier known as* D. caesius*) grows about 20cm/8in high and spreads to 30cm/12in or more. The fragrant, fringed, pink flowers appear from late spring to mid-summer.*

• *Dianthus alpinus* (Alpine Pink), 10cm/4in high and about 15cm/6in wide, forms mats of deep green leaves. From late spring to late summer it develops pale pink to purple flowers, each with a white eye. There is also a white-flowered form. Unfortunately, it is rather short-lived and new plants need to be raised every couple of years.

• *Dianthus deltoides* (Maiden Pink) is an old and well-established favourite, about 20cm/8in high and with a similar spread. The leaves are narrow, and mid to dark green, while the early summer to early autumn flowers range in colour from red to white. It is an ideal plant for positioning in crevices between rocks and for planting between paving stones.

• *Dianthus neglectus* (also known as *D. pavonius*), 10–20cm/4–8in high and about 15cm/6in across, forms tufts of grey-green leaves. It is a variable species and creates masses of flowers during mid and late summer. These range from pale pink to deep crimson.

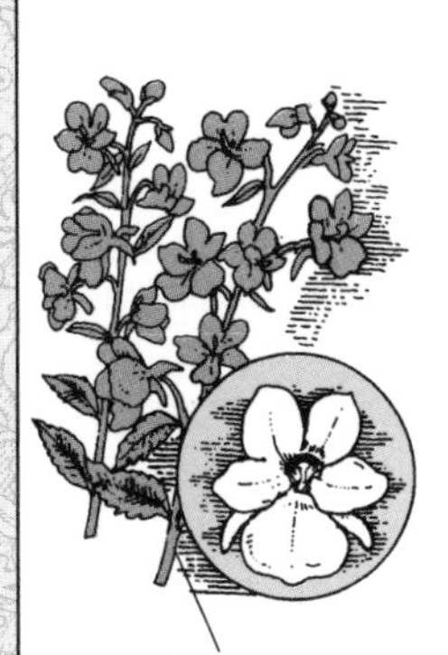

DIASCIA *'Ruby Field', about 23cm/9in high and with the same spread, develops ruby-coloured flowers from late spring to mid-summer. Pinch out the tips of shoots to encourage it to become bushy.*

DODECATHEON MEADIA *(Shooting Star), 30–45cm/12–18in high and 25cm/10in wide, is best reserved for large rock gardens. Rose-purple flowers appear during late spring and into the early part of summer.*

EDRAIANTHUS SERPYLLIFOLIUS *forms a mat of deep green leaves about 2.5cm/1in high and spreads to 23cm/9in. In early summer it develops purple flowers at the tips of stems.*

ROCK-GARDEN PERENNIALS
Erinus – Iberis

GENTIANS are popular rock garden plants, often creating vast sheets of colour. In addition to those illustrated here, there are many others to consider.

- *Gentiana farreri*, 10cm/4in high and spreading to 25cm/10in, is one of the best for a rock garden. From late summer to mid-autumn, the narrow, lance-shaped, light green leaves become awash with blue, trumpet-like flowers with white throats.
- *Gentiana gracilipes*, 15–23cm/6–9in high and spreading to 38cm/15in, forms tufts of narrow mid-green leaves. During mid and late summer, branching stems bear funnel-shaped purple flowers that are striped with green.

ERINUS ALPINUS *(Summer Starwort), 7.5cm/3in high and spreading to 15cm/6in, forms evergreen tufts of mid-green leaves and starry, bright pink flowers from early spring to late summer. It is ideal for planting in a scree.*

FRANKENIA THYMAEFOLIA *(Sea Heath), about 7.5cm/3in high and quickly spreading to form a mat, is covered in clear pink flowers during mid-spring and late summer. Use well-drained soil and a position in full sun.*

GENTIANA ACAULIS *(Trumpet Gentian) grows 7.5cm/3in high and spreads to 38cm/15in. During late spring and early summer it produces deep blue flowers, up to 7.5cm/3in long. They stand clear above the mats of mid-green leaves.*

UNGRATEFUL PLANT

The Yellow Gentian or Gentian Root (Gentiana lutea) *was probably the first cultivated gentian to be introduced from Europe into England. It was then called Baldmoney, Bitterwort or Felwort, known for its medicinal qualities and used to flavour liqueurs. It grows about 1m/3½ft high and when grown by nineteenth-century gardeners proved so difficult that it was said to signify ingratitude. The gentian family was named in honour of Gentius, King of Illyria, an ancient region in the Balkans.*

GENTIANA VERNA *(Spring Gentian) grows 7.5cm/3in high and spreads to 15cm/6in. During late spring and early summer it develops 2.5cm/1in-long, blue flowers. Well-drained, chalky soil is essential for this plant.*

GERANIUM 'Ballerina', *a hybrid about 20cm/8in high and spreading to 30cm/12in, has pink flowers up to 2.5cm/1in wide, from early to late summer. The flowers are heavily veined in deep pink and the leaves are lobed.*

GERANIUM SUBCAULESCENS, *10–15cm/4–6in high and spreading to 30cm/12in or more. From late spring to mid-autumn it bears 2.5cm/1in-wide, bright crimson-magenta flowers. There are several other forms.*

• *Gentiana septemfida*, 23cm/9in high and spreading to 30cm/12in, is easily grown but only suitable for large rock gardens. From mid to late summer it produces clusters of 3.6cm/1½in-long, purple-blue trumpet-shaped flowers.

• *Gentiana sino-ornata* is a superb autumn-flowering species. It is about 15cm/6in high and spreads to 38cm/15in, with bright blue, trumpet-shaped flowers from early autumn to early winter. The 5cm/2in-long trumpets are striped in pale green.

• *Gentiana 'Stevenagensis'*, 10cm/4in high and spreading to 30cm/12in, produces 5cm/2in-high, rich blue trumpets during late summer and early autumn.

GEUM MONTANUM *grows 15–30cm/6–12in high and with a 23–30cm/9–12in spread. From late spring to mid-summer it produces yellow flowers.*

GYPSOPHILA REPENS (G. prostrata), *grows up to 15cm/6in high and spreads to 45cm/18in. From early to late summer it bears white to pink flowers.*

IBERIS SEMPERVIRENS *'Little Gem' (Perennial Candytuft), 10cm/4in high and spreading to 23cm/9in, has white flowers during late spring and early summer.*

ROCK-GARDEN PERENNIALS
Leontopodium - Omphalodes

LEWISIAS are popular rock-garden plants and native to the western states of North America. Most of them form an evergreen rosette of semi-succulent leaves; some have thick, starchy, edible roots. They all need well-drained soil, as water that remains at their centre during winter quickly causes decay. Plant them in crevices between rocks. When planted in other positions, surround them with a mulch of stone chippings. Covering them with small glass tents also helps to keep them dry during winter. There are many species to choose from and one of them, *Leontopodium alpinum*, is illustrated here. Others include:

- *Lewisia brachycalyx*, up to 7.5cm/3in high and spreading to 20cm/ 8in, has a rosette of fleshy leaves from which flower stems develop. The shiny white or pinkish flowers appear late in spring.
- *Lewisia tweedyi*, 15cm/6in high and spreading to 23cm/9in, is evergreen, with loose rosettes of mid-green leaves and 5cm/2in-wide, pale-pink flowers during mid and late spring.
- *Lewisia rediviva* (Bitter Root), 7.5cm/3in high and spreading to 15cm/6in, forms a rosette which dies during early summer when 5cm/2in-wide white or rose-pink flowers appear.

LEONTOPODIUM ALPINUM *(Edelweiss), 20cm/ 8in high and spreading to 23cm/ 9in, reveals grey-green leaves and white flowers surrounded by woolly bracts in early and mid-summer.*

PERENNIAL FLAX

Choose from a wide range of Linums:

- *Linum perenne*, an herbaceous perennial with blue flowers, is illustrated on the opposite page.
- *Linum narbonense* 'Heavenly Blue' has an herbaceous nature – sometimes evergreen in mild areas – growing to 38cm/15in high and spreading to 30cm/12in. Between early summer and early autumn it produces rich blue flowers with white centres.

AGE-OLD PLANT

The flax now known as Linum usitatissimum *and widely called the Common Flax or Linseed is claimed to be one of the first plants to become associated with man. Indeed, its second name implies 'the most useful', while flax is derived from the Old English* fleaux, *meaning to braid or interweave. It was cultivated during early antiquity in Egypt for its fibre, later in India, Argentina and China for its seed that yields Linseed Oil.*

This flax, a graceful annual, with pale blue flowers in early and mid-summer, has many traditions: in the Middle Ages the flowers were thought to offer protection against sorcery.

LINARIA ALPINA *(Alpine Toadflax), 7.5–15cm/ 3–6in high and spreading to 23cm/ 9in, has sprays of violet flowers from early to late summer.*

LEWISIA COTYLEDON, *with a dense rosette of mid-green, fleshy, spoon-shaped leaves, develops clusters of star-like, pink flowers on 20cm/ 8in stems during late spring and early summer.*

LINUM PERENNE ALPINUM *(Alpine Flax), about 15cm/ 6in high and spreading to 20cm/ 8in, has blue flowers from early to late summer. They fade quickly, but are renewed.*

LITHOSPERMUM DIFFUSUM *(often sold as* Lithodora diffusa*), is 15cm/ 6in high and spreads to 60cm/ 2ft. It has blue flowers in summer. 'Heavenly Blue' and 'Grace Ward' are popular.*

LYCHNIS ALPINA ROSEA *(Alpine Campion), grows about 10cm/ 4in high and with a similar spread. It has deep pink flowers from late spring to mid-summer. There is also a white form.*

OENOTHERA MISSOURIENSIS *(Ozark Sundrops) is 15cm/ 6in high and spreads to 45cm/ 1½ft. Yellow flowers up to 7.5cm/ 3in appear in summer.*

OMPHALODES VERNA *(Blue-eyed Mary), is 15cm/ 6in high and spreads to 30cm/ 12in. From early to late spring it has bright blue, white-throated flowers.*

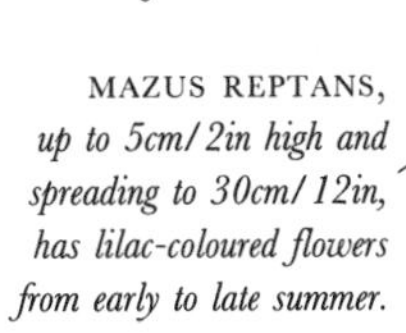

MAZUS REPTANS, *up to 5cm/ 2in high and spreading to 30cm/ 12in, has lilac-coloured flowers from early to late summer.*

ROCK-GARDEN PERENNIALS

Ourisia – Primula

THE wealth of plants which can be grown in rock gardens is wide and in addition to those featured here there are many others to consider.

- *Oxalis enneaphylla*, 7.5cm/3in high and spreading to 15cm/6in, creates hummocks of grey, partially folded leaves. During early and mid-summer these are covered with 2.5cm/1in-wide, funnel-shaped white flowers.
- *Oxalis magellanica*, 5cm/2in high and spreading to 30cm/12in, forms a mat of bronze leaves. The white, cup-shaped flowers appear during late spring and early summer.
- *Papaver alpinum*, a short-lived perennial, is about 20cm/8in high and spreads to 15cm/6in. It is ideal in a rock garden or scree bed where, from late spring to mid-summer, it displays flowers in a range of colours from white to yellow and red above mounds of deeply dissected grey-green leaves.

POPPY POWER

The poppy family includes many different types of plants, such as annuals, biennials and herbaceous perennials. Papaver alpinum *is ideal for growing in rock gardens, together with* P. miyabeanum *(Japanese Alpine Poppy). But it is the Opium Poppy* (P. somniferum) *and Field Poppy* (P. rhoeas), *both annuals, that are first remembered when poppies are discussed. And it is the Field Poppy that is used as a symbol of Remembrance.*

- *Phlox subulata* (Moss Phlox) is 10–13cm/4–5in high and spreads to 38cm/15in. It has a sub-shrubby nature and forms a mat of narrow, mid-green leaves. During mid and late spring it is smothered in pink or purple flowers.

OURISIA COCCINEA, *15–30cm/6–12in high and spreading to 45cm/18in or more, creates dense mats of mid-green leaves. From late spring to autumn it bears tubular, scarlet flowers on erect stems.*

OXALIS ADENOPHYLLA, *7.5cm/3in high and with a 15cm/6in spread, has crinkled, grey-green, pleated leaves and cup-shaped, 2.5cm/1in-wide, satin-pink flowers with veining from late spring to mid-summer.*

PARAHEBE LYALII, *about 20cm/8in high and spreading to 25cm/10in, has leathery, green leaves and white flowers with pink veins during mid and late summer. It is easier to grow than most other plants in this genus.*

PENSTEMON ROEZLII, *from the western states of North America, is 10–23cm/ 4–9in high and spreads to 30cm/ 12in. It is smothered in lavender to violet-blue flowers in clusters during mid-summer. It has narrow, lance-shaped, mid-green leaves.*

POLYGONUM AFFINE *'Donald Lowndes', 15–23cm/ 6–9in high and spreading to 45cm/ 18in, develops into a mat of spoon-shaped leaves (bright green when young but later brown), and rosy-red flowers during early summer.*

PHLOX DOUGLASII *(Alpine Phlox), 5–10cm/ 2–4in high and spreading to 45cm/ 18in, reveals masses of pale-lavender flowers during late spring and early summer. There are many varieties, in colours including pink and white.*

There are several varieties, including 'Scarlet Flame' (scarlet) and 'Temiscaming' (pale red).

- *Pleione bulbocodioides* (also known as *P. formosana*), 15cm/ 6in high and about the same width when in flower, creates 7.5–10cm/3–4in-wide trumpets in white to mauve-pink during mid and late spring. Most pleiones are not suitable for growing outdoors in a rock garden, but this species is ideal if the soil is well drained and the situation sheltered.

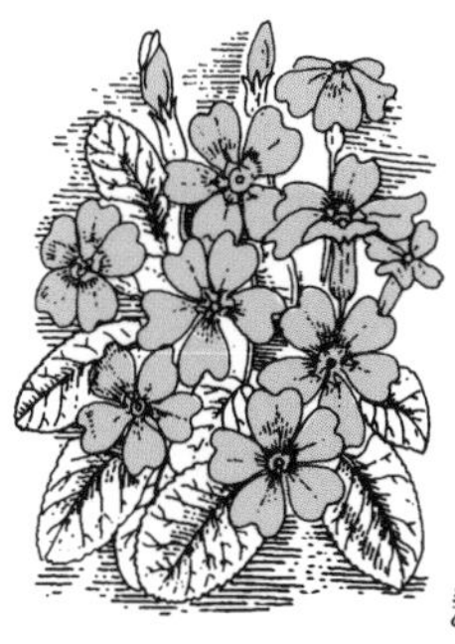

POTENTILLA AUREA *(Golden Cinquefoil), 10cm/ 4in high and spreading to 30cm/ 12in, forms a bright mound of shiny yellow flowers from early summer to the frosts of autumn. It is mat-forming and ideal when creeping over rocks.*

PRIMULA *'Wanda' is a superb hybrid alpine primula, 10–15cm/ 4–6in high and with the same spread. It flowers during mid and late spring, revealing purple-red flowers in clusters above large, spoon-shaped, shiny mid-green leaves.*

PRIMULA VIALII, *which grows up to 30cm/ 12in high and with a 23–30cm/ 10–12in spread, creates poker-like heads of lavender-blue flowers during early and mid-summer. These are borne above large, pale green, spoon-shaped leaves.*

ROCK-GARDEN PERENNIALS
Pulsatilla – Sedum

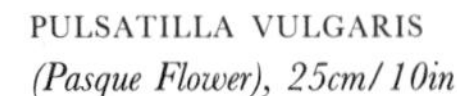

THE range of rock-garden perennials continues, with some that have a delicate nature in wet, temperate climates and therefore need cosseting. Examples of these plants include:

- *Raoulia hookeri* (also known as *R. australis*) forms mats of silvery leaves no more than 12mm/½in high and spreading to 30cm/12in. During late spring it reveals rather insignificant yellow flowers.
- *Raoulia eximia* (Vegetable Sheep), up to 7.5cm/3in high and spreading to 30cm/12in, forms silvery-white hummocks. It is only suitable outdoors in a sunny position and well-drained soil.
- *Raoulia lutescens*, about 12mm/½in high and spreading to 45cm/18in, forms mats of grey-green leaves. During mid and late spring these are peppered with minute, lemon-yellow flowers.

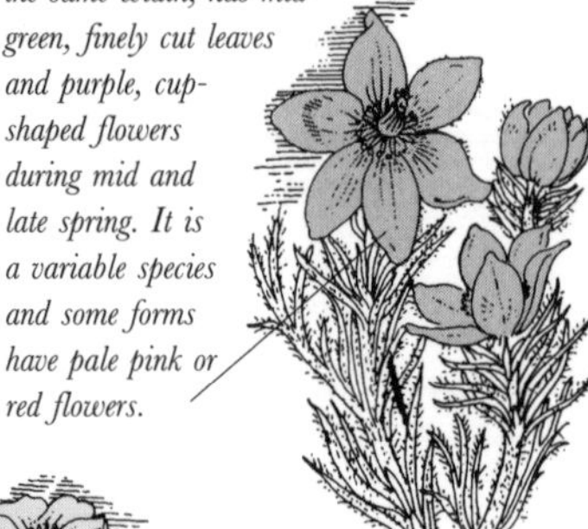

PULSATILLA VULGARIS *(Pasque Flower), 25cm/10in high and spreading to about the same width, has mid-green, finely cut leaves and purple, cup-shaped flowers during mid and late spring. It is a variable species and some forms have pale pink or red flowers.*

RANUNCULUS GRAMINEUS, *25–30cm/10–12in high and with a similar spread, has narrow, grey-green leaves and loose sprays of bright, golden-yellow flowers from late spring to mid-summer.*

SANGUINARIA CANADENSIS *'Flore Pleno' (Bloodroot), 15cm/6in high and spreading to 30cm/12in, has pale-green, lobed leaves and petal-packed white flowers during mid and late-spring. It is ideal in peat beds.*

SAPONARIA OCYMOIDES, *7.5cm/3in high and spreading to 30cm/12in, is ground-hugging. From mid-summer to autumn it bears rose-pink flowers. 'Rubra Compacta' has reddish-pink flowers and is compact.*

SAXIFRAGA AIZOON *(now correctly* S. paniculata*), 10cm/25cm high and wide, with sprays of white, star-shaped flowers borne in graceful sprays during mid-summer. The lance-shaped leaves are silver-green and form rosettes.*

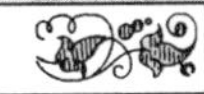

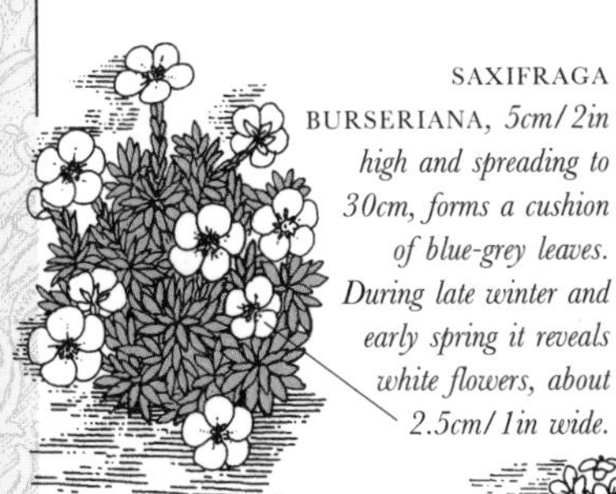

SAXIFRAGA BURSERIANA, *5cm/2in high and spreading to 30cm, forms a cushion of blue-grey leaves. During late winter and early spring it reveals white flowers, about 2.5cm/1in wide.*

• *Ramonda myconi* (also known as *R. pyrenaica*), 10–15cm/4–6in high and about 23cm/9in wide, forms a rosette of evergreen, deep green and hairy leaves. During mid and late spring stems about 10cm/4in long bear flat-faced, lavender-blue flowers, each with a central cone of yellow stamens. There are many forms, such as 'Alba' (white), 'Rosea' (pink) and 'Coerulea' (blue).

• *Rhodohypoxis baurii*, about 7.5cm/3in high and spreading to 15cm/6in, is a South African perennial. The narrow, hairy, pale green leaves become smothered with rosy-red flowers from mid-spring to early autumn. There are several varieties, extending the flower colour to white, pink and purple. Well-drained but moisture-retentive soil is essential, together with protection in winter.

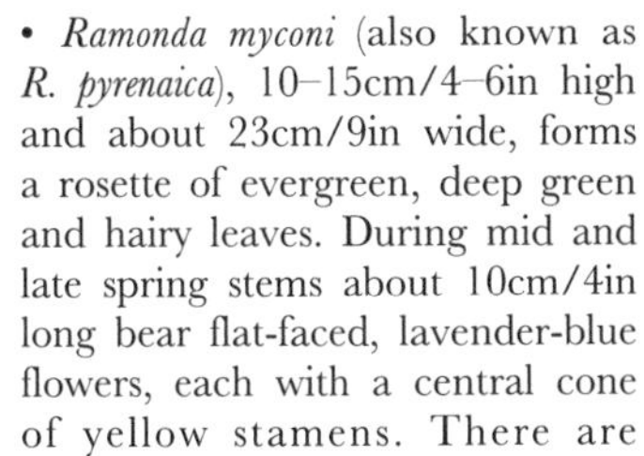

SAXIFRAGA COCHLEARIS *'Minor', 10cm/4in high and spreading to 20cm/8in, forms compact, silver hummocks and sprays of white flowers during early summer. It is ideal for planting in rock crevices.*

PASQUE FLOWER

For many years this hardy European plant with finely cut, fern-like leaves was known as Anemone pulsatilla. *It is claimed to have gained the name Pasque Flower from the Old French* pasques, *meaning Easter and referring to its flowering period; while pulsatilla derives from* pulsare, *meaning to shake or beat, and dates from classical times when the flowers appeared to be shaken by the wind. Earlier, this plant was praised for its medicinal value, being considered a cure for arthritis. But it is poisonous and at one time was known as Laughing Parsley because it was said that people eating it would die of laughter!*

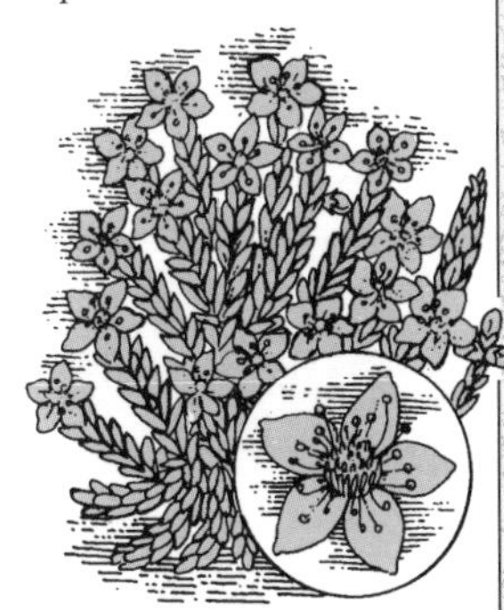

SAXIFRAGA COTYLEDON *'Southside Seedling', about 25cm/10in high and 20cm/8in wide, forms a basal rosette of strap-like leaves. During early and mid-summer it develops arching sprays of white flowers, heavily spotted red. It is ideal for planting in crevices.*

SEDUM ACRE *'Aureum' (Biting Stonecrop), up to 5cm/2in high and spreading to 30cm/12in or more, forms a mat of yellowish-green leaves. During early and mid-summer it develops flattened heads of yellow flowers. It spreads attractively over the bases of rocks.*

ROCK-GARDEN PERENNIALS

Sedum – Thymus

MANY sedums are bright-faced, reliable and easily grown plants for rock gardens.

- *Sedum acre* (Biting Stonecrop), 2.5–5cm/1–2in high and spreading to 38cm/15in, is evergreen and forms a mat of mid-green succulent leaves. During early and mid-summer these are smothered in flat heads of yellow flowers.
- *Sedum ewersii*, 10–15cm/4–6in high, spreading to 45cm/18in and with a trailing nature, has grey-green leaves and pink or red flowers during late summer.
- *Sedum kamtschaticum* 'Variegatum', about 15cm/6in high and spreading to 30cm/12in, has distinctive dark green, succulent leaves edged cream and red. The flowers are golden yellow.

HOUSELEEKS

These are sempervivums and one of the species that is suitable for a rock garden is featured and illustrated below. Others include:

- *Sempervivum montanum*, about 2.5cm/1in high and spreading to 23cm/9in, forms dull green rosettes up to 5cm/2in across. From early to late summer it develops reddish-purple flowers on stems about 13cm/5in high.
- *Sempervivum soboliferum* (also known as *Jovibarba sobolifera* and commonly as Hen and Chicken Houseleek) is about 2.5cm/1in high and spreads to 25cm/10in or more. The rosettes are formed of bright green leaves, flushed red, and surmounted during mid-summer by yellow, bell-like flowers.

SEDUM SPATHUIFOLIUM *'Cappa Blanca', 5–10cm/2–4in high, spreading to 23cm/9in. Yellow flowers appear in early summer.*

SEDUM SPURIUM, *about 10cm/4in high and spreading to 30cm/12in, has rich pink flowers during mid and late summer.*

SEMPERVIVUM ARACHNOIDEUM *(Cobweb Plant/Houseleek), about 2.5cm/1in high and spreading to 25cm/10in. Rosy-red flowers appear in early and mid-summer.*

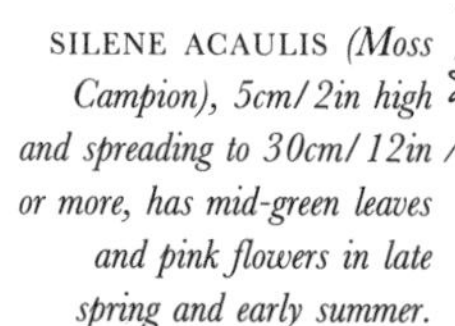

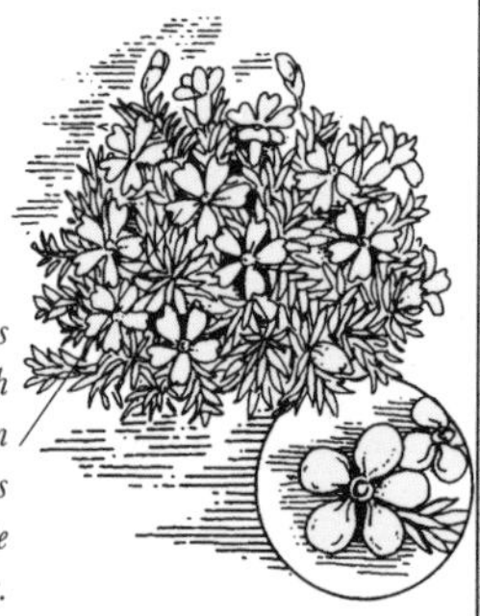

SILENE ACAULIS *(Moss Campion), 5cm/2in high and spreading to 30cm/12in or more, has mid-green leaves and pink flowers in late spring and early summer.*

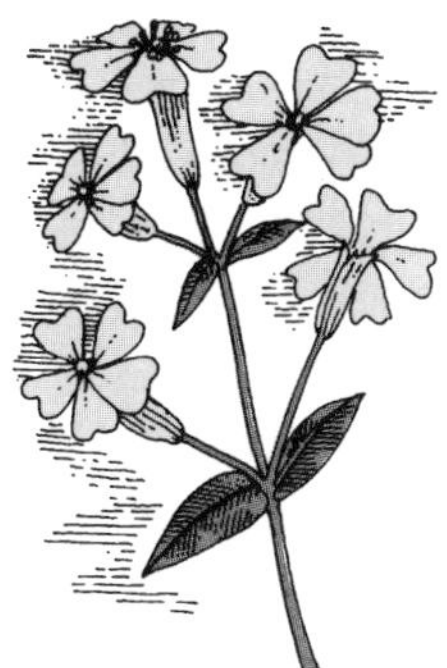

SILENE SCHAFTA, *10–15cm/4–6in high and spreading to 30cm/12in, forms tufts of lance-shaped, mid-green leaves. From mid-summer to early autumn it develops sprays of bright, magenta-pink flowers on 10–15cm/4–6in-long stems. It is an easily grown species and forms spreading mats and tufts.*

SISYRINCHIUM BERMUDIANUM *(Blue-eye Grass), 15–23cm/6–9in high and about the same wide, forms clumps of erect, stiff, grass-like leaves. During late spring and early summer it develops star-shaped, light blue flowers with yellow bases. It is native to North America and the western part of Ireland.*

THYMUS *X* CITRIODORUS *(Lemon-scented Thyme), about 23cm/9in high and spreading to 38cm/15in, forms a mat of mid-green, lemon-scented leaves. Pale lilac flowers appear during summer. Varieties include 'Silver Queen' with silver-green, variegated leaves, illustrated above.*

THYMUS SERPYLLUM *(Wild Thyme), up to 7.5cm/3in high and spreading to 45cm/18in or more, with narrow, grey-green and sometimes hairy leaves. Flowers appear from early to late summer, in a range of colours. There are several superb varieties, including 'Annie Hall' (pale pink), 'Coccineus' (rich crimson) and 'Albus' (white).*

WALL SITTERS

Even the Latin sedum, *meaning plant that sits, gives a clue to the nature of most of the plants in this genus. There are a few species, such as the Ice Plant* (Sedum spectabilis) *and Orpine* (S. telephium), *that are best in an herbaceous border, but most prefer to sit on natural stone walls or to live in a rock garden. The yellow-flowered Biting Stonecrop* (S. acre) *is a scrambler and known to the herbalist and barber-surgeon, John Gerard, in the late sixteenth century as Wall-pepper, Iacke-of-the-Butterie and Pricket.*

The Stone Orpine (S. reflexum) *was eaten in Holland in salads, the leaves having a pleasant taste, while the seventeenth-century French botanist, Joseph Tournefort, considered it good for 'hartburne'.*

ROCK-GARDEN PERENNIALS

Verbascum – Wadsteinia

Few rock garden plants have the simplicity yet the extraordinary fascination revealed by violas. Apart from the dramatic appeal of Garden Pansies (*Viola* x *wittrockiana*), with their large faces and wide colour range, there are many others.

- *Viola bifolia*, 5–7.5cm/2–3in high and spreading to 30cm/12in, has bright green, kidney-shaped leaves and yellow, violet-like flowers during mid and late spring.
- *Viola gracilis*, 10cm/4in high and spreading to 25cm/10in or more, has deep purple flowers about 2.5cm/1in in width from mid-spring to early summer. These flowers have a pansy-like outline, with various varieties increasing the colour range to purple-black and yellow.
- *Viola labradorica* 'Purpurea', about 10cm/4in high and spreading to 30cm/12in or more, has mid-green leaves that assume a purple tinge. During mid and late spring it develops mauve-coloured, violet-like flowers.

GARDEN PANSIES

These are hybrids and varieties of *Viola* x *wittrockiana*. To the rock-garden purist they may be too brazen and rich in colour to be considered as partners for demure alpines, but in a new rock garden they offer nearly instant colour. And these seed-raised plants can be removed later if they have offended too many eyes.

There are both summer and winter-flowering varieties. The summer ones bloom from late spring to early autumn, while winter ones flower from early winter to late spring. Each year new varieties are introduced: choose low-growing types as they harmonize with other plants.

VERBASCUM DUMULOSUM, *20–30cm/8–12in high and about the same in width, has a shrubby nature with grey-green and slightly woolly leaves. During early and mid-summer it produces clusters of clear yellow flowers.*

VERBASCUM *'Letitia', 15–20cm/6–8in high and spreading to 30cm/12in or more, forms a diminutive shrublet with lance-shaped, grey-green leaves and spikes of clear, bright yellow flowers from early to late summer.*

VERONICA PECTINATA, *7.5cm/3in high and spreading to 30cm/12in or more, has a prostrate nature with toothed, grey-green leaves. During late spring and early summer it has deep blue flowers with a white eye. 'Rosea' has pink flowers.*

VERONICA PROSTRATA *(also sold as* V. rupestris *and* V. teucrium prostrata*), grows 10–15cm/4–6in high and with a spread of 30cm/12in or more. From late spring to mid-summer the mid-green leaves are smothered with deep blue flowers in spires.*

VIOLA CORNUTA *(Horned Pansy/Horned Viola), 15–23cm/6–9in high and spreading to 38cm/45in, has mid-green leaves and deep lavender flowers about 2.5cm/1in wide during early and mid-summer. Several varieties include 'Alba' (white).*

VIOLA LUTEA, *15–20cm/6–8in high and spreading to about 23cm/9in, forms mats of mid-green leaves. During early and mid-summer it produces bright-faced, yellow flowers which seldom fail to attract attention. It is one of the most easily grown violas.*

GREAT MULLEIN

Few plants have collected as many common names as the Great Mullein (Verbascum thapsus)*. These include Yellow Mullein, Clown's Lungwort, Candlewick Plant and Hag's Taper. It is found wild in Europe and temperate Asia, as well as North America, although it is doubtful if it is a true native of that area.*

Its uses are wide; the poor were said to have put the thick, woolly leaves in their shoes to create extra warmth; the Romans dipped the stems in tallow and used them as torches; witches used them in sorcery; while the juice of the leaves and flowers when put on warts eased their removal. As well, the seeds, when put in ponds, are said to stupefy fish so that they can be removed by hand. Earlier, it was used to treat cattle, and was therefore called Bullock's Lungwort.

WALDSTEINIA FRAGARIOIDES *(Barren Strawberry) has strawberry-like, dark green and three-lobed leaves. Plants grow about 15cm/6in high and spread to 25cm/10in. During early summer it has golden-yellow flowers on stems 10–13cm/4–5in high. If it becomes invasive and likely to swamp other plants, clip it back in spring.*

PESTS AND DISEASES

REGULARLY inspecting plants, especially in spring when young shoots and leaves appear, is important. In autumn, clear away rubbish that might harbour pests and diseases. A mulch of small stone chippings or pea-shingle around plants both encourages better drainage and deters slugs and snails from crawling over the ground and reaching plants.

Do not feed plants excessively, especially after the latter part of mid-summer, as it causes lush growth which is susceptible to diseases and pests.

When cats, birds and moles are a problem there is always a temptation to overreact and to consider preventative measures that might kill rather than deter them. To varying degrees, all birds are protected by the law, while unnecessary stress to any animal is not acceptable. Indeed, it is possible that such treatment of animals could lead to prosecution.

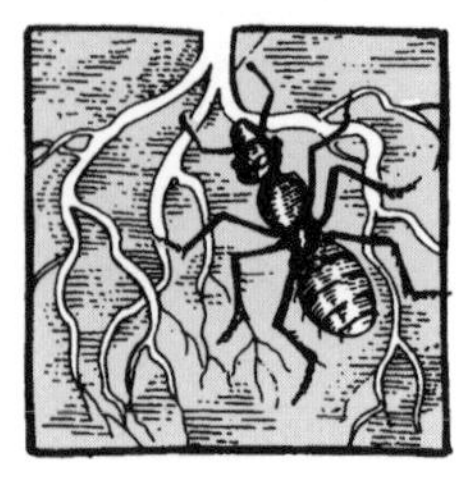

ANTS *are sometimes a problem in rock gardens; they cluster in soil around plants, loosening it and disturbing roots. Their presence is encouraged by aphids. Use an ant killer.*

APHIDS *(greenfly) suck sap from young shoots and flowers, causing weakening and distortion. They excrete honeydew which encourages ants. Use a systemic insecticide.*

BIRDS *such as blackbirds, sparrows and bullfinches devastate plants in spring. Humane prevention is difficult: black cotton strung across susceptible plants is the best way.*

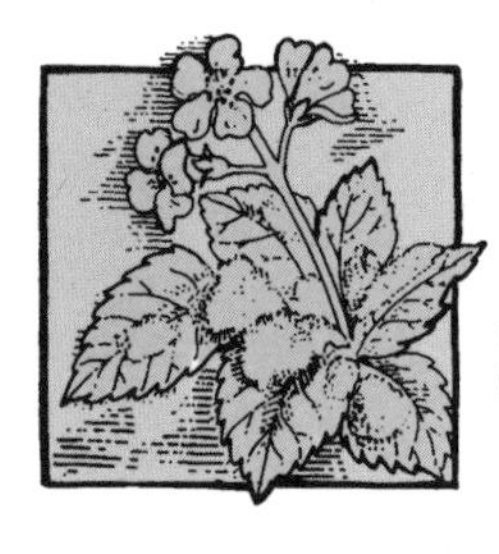

BOTRYTIS *(greymould) forms a fluffy, grey mould over leaves, stems and flowers. Too close planting and poor circulation of air encourages it. Pick off and destroy infected parts and use a systemic fungicide.*

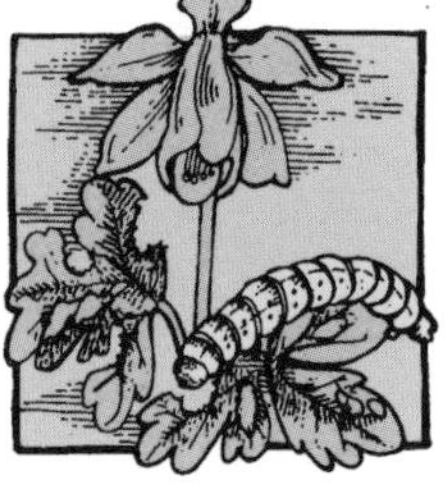

CATERPILLARS *chew leaves, peppering them with large holes. Inspect plants and pick off caterpillars, but if the infestation is severe, spray with an insecticide. If a plant becomes ravaged, remove and burn it.*

CATS *like digging up light, well-drained soil. Dusting soil with pepper is often recommended. A 2.5cm/1in mulch of pea-shingle gives cats something to scratch before they reach and damage the roots.*

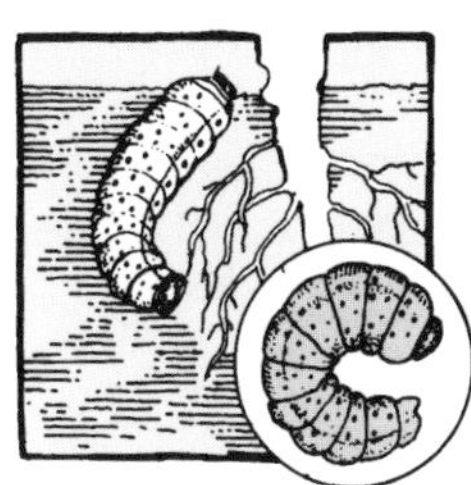

CUTWORMS *are the larvae of some moths; they chew the roots of seedlings and young plants, causing their collapse. Dust the soil with an insecticide. Regularly hoe around plants.*

MICE *in search of food often dig down in winter to feed on bulbs and corms, especially during severe weather. The best protection is to cover bulbs with wire netting, pegged on the surface.*

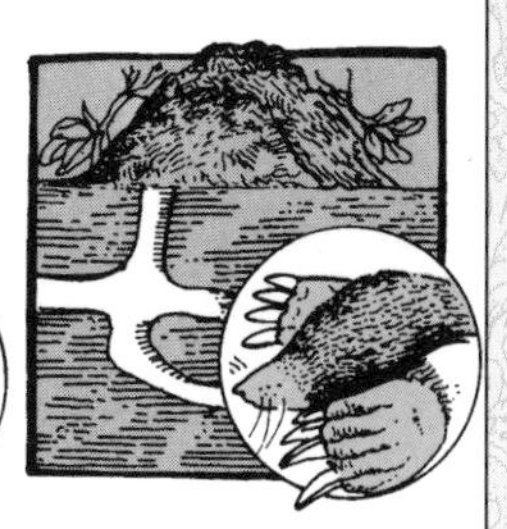

MOLES *are tenacious pests in rock gardens as plants cannot easily be moved out of the way of their tunnels. Block up runs with slate. Do not use metal traps, as they are cruel.*

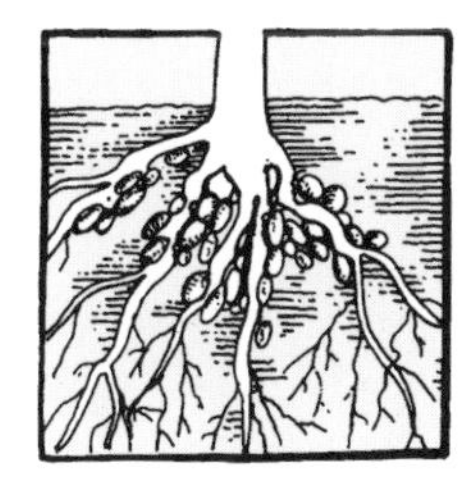

ROOT APHIDS *are pests in warm areas; they graze on roots, causing wilting and discoloration. The only solution is to drench the soil with an insecticide. They also may be a problem in alpine houses in summer.*

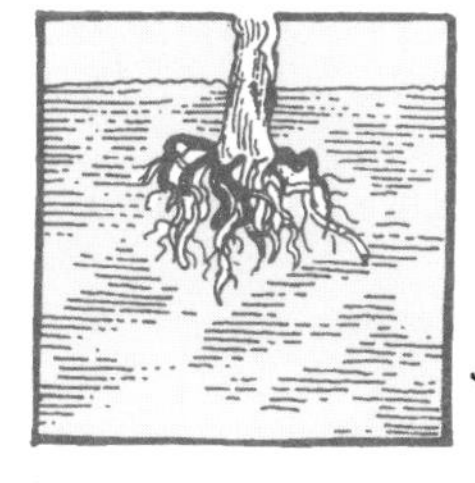

ROOT ROTS *are encouraged by wet, cold soil. This should not occur in rock gardens, but as most of these plants are native to well-drained soil, even the smallest excess of moisture troubles some of them.*

SLUGS *have voracious appetites in late spring and early summer and are especially troublesome during warm periods. A shingle mulch deters them, or use slug baits. In addition, pick them off and destroy them.*

SNAILS, *like slugs, are also a problem in spring and can soon devastate plants. Prevent and kill them in the same way. Additionally, pick up and compost all dead leaves and flowers. Also, improve the drainage.*

SOOTY MOULD *is a fungus that lives on honey-dew excreted by aphids. It blackens stems and leaves, making them unsightly. Spray regularly to kill the aphids. Pull off and destroy badly affected leaves.*

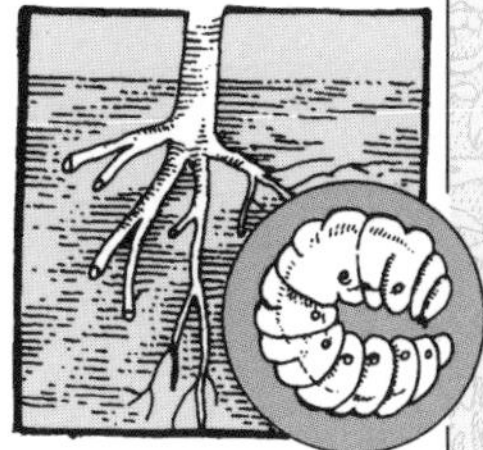

VINE WEEVILS *are small, usually curled, white grubs of vine-weevil beetles. They chew roots, causing plants to wilt and die. If a plant wilts unexpectedly, check if they are present. Drench the soil with an insecticide.*

ROCK-GARDEN CALENDAR

SPRING

This is the time of most activity in rock gardens.

- Spring is the best time to start constructing rock-garden features (8–9). These range from rock gardens on slopes to dry-stone walls and converting glazed sinks into attractive containers (13–19.
- Prepare the foundations for raised beds and dry-stone walls as soon as the risk of frost has passed (14–15).
- Dig out the area of scree beds as soon as the soil is workable and there is no risk of water draining into it (16). If drainage is poor, install drains.
- Construct peat beds in woodland with light shade. Compressed peat blocks and peat are needed, and logs or old railway sleepers if there is a large amount of soil to be constrained (16–17).
- Convert glazed sinks into attractive containers as soon as there is no risk of frost (18–19).
- In late spring, plant small plants in gaps between natural stone paving slabs (15).
- Thoroughly inspect all plants before buying them (20).
- Pull up weeds as soon as they appear (20–21). If this task is neglected and the weeds grow large, their eventual removal unnecessarily disturbs the soil and roots of rock garden plants.
- In late spring or early summer, lift and divide clumps of congested plants (20–21).
- Plant rock-garden plants as soon as the soil is workable (20–21).
- Feed plants in late spring or early summer (20–21).
- Form a mulch of stone chippings or pea-shingle around plants in late spring (20–21).

SUMMER

- Early summer is a good time to start to construct rock gardens on slopes (12–13).
- Prepare the foundations for raised beds and dry-stone walls as soon as the soil is dry. This can also be tackled in late spring, but if the weather is frosty it is better delayed until early summer. However, never lay concrete when the weather is exceptionally hot (14–15).
- Dig out the area of scree beds as soon as the soil is workable and there is no risk of water draining into it (16). If drainage is poor, it is essential to install some drains.
- Construct peat beds in woodland. Compressed peat blocks and peat are needed, and logs or old railway sleepers if there is a large amount of soil to be supported (16–17).
- Convert glazed sinks into attractive containers (18–19).
- In early summer, plant small plants between natural paving slabs (15).
- Inspect all plants before buying them (20).
- Pull up weeds as soon as they appear (20–21).
- In late spring, or early summer, carefully lift and divide congested plants (20–21).
- Plant healthy new rock-garden plants as soon as the soil is workable (20–21).
- Feed plants in late spring or early summer (20–21).
- Water newly planted rock-garden plants (20–21).
- During dry periods, water rock-garden plants (20–21).
- Form a mulch of stone chippings or pea-shingle around plants in early summer (20–21).
- Remove dead flowers (20–21).

AUTUMN

This is the time for clearing up rock gardens, removing leaves and other debris. In addition, dead leaves and faded flowers must also be removed. All of this is to prevent dampness remaining around plants that, by nature, are susceptible to decay.

Clear up peat beds, again removing leaves and other debris. If late summer or early autumn has been exceptionally dry, keep the peat blocks and compost moist. Once the peat has been allowed to become very dry, the plants suffer and it is difficult to re-moisten it.

- Many spring-flowering bulbs can be planted in late summer or early autumn. Prepare the soil and plant them in the way described on pages 24–25. Additionally, the distances to space individual bulbs are given on pages 24–27.
- Where mice are persistent pests during winter, cover the area where bulbs have been planted with wire netting (58–59). Peg it on the surface and ensure the ends are buried. In mild winters, mice are not so much of a problem to plants.
- Pull up weeds as soon as they appear (20–21). If this task is neglected and the weeds grow large, their eventual removal disturbs the soil and roots of established plants.
- Quickly remove leaves that fall on plants (20–21). If left, they cause moisture to remain around plants.
- Tidy up plants in autumn, burning diseased and pest-infected parts (20–21).
- If the weather is exceptionally cold and wet, protect plants by propping up pieces of glass over them. Alternatively, use small cloches (20).

WINTER

This is the time for reflection and planning. Regularly check the rock garden to ensure plants are safe, glass tents over tender plants are secure and that the area is free from rubbish.

Now is the time to plan for changes and new plants. Inspect specialist catalogues and order plants as soon as possible to avoid disappointment later.

If an extension to your rock garden is being planned, regularly check that the area is not waterlogged. If the feature is to be a scree bed, dig a hole 45–60cm/ 1–1½ft deep and monitor the amount of water resting in it. If the level remains within 30cm/ 12in of the surface, the installation of drains is essential.

If falling leaves were a problem in autumn, it may have been the result of branches from nearby trees encroaching over the area. Winter is the best time to cut off branches, but check that you are legally entitled to do this. Also, only tackle branch lopping and tree felling when the weather is dry. It may be better to call in professional tree surgeons.

- In early winter, protect tender alpines by propping up pieces of glass over them. Alternatively, use small cloches (20).
- During winter, plan the position of a rock garden. It is essential to consider the position and aspect carefully (10–11).
- Check with local suppliers of rock to gain an idea of the cost of stone (10–11).
- Assess the amount of stone needed to construct a rock garden (10–11).
- Do not sprinkle salt or sand on natural stone paths which have plants growing in the cracks between the slabs. It may kill the plants (19).

GLOSSARY OF ROCK-GARDEN TERMS

ACID: *Refers to soil that has a pH below 7.0. Most plants grow best in slightly acid soil, about 6.5.*

ALKALINE: *Having a chalky nature and a pH reading above 7.0.*

ALPINE: *A plant that grows between the permanent snow line on a mountain and the uppermost limit of trees.*

ALPINE HOUSE: *A greenhouse used to protect alpine plants from excessive moisture. Usually it is unheated but well ventilated.*

ALPINE LAWN: *Instead of using grass to form a lawn, plants like Wild Thyme* (Thymus serpyllum) *are used. Clearly, it is more for decoration and to form a background for other plants than a hard-wearing area.*

ANNUAL: *A plant that completes its life-cycle within a single season. Seeds are sown, they germinate, grow and produce flowers and seeds within the same year.*

BIENNIAL: *A plant that is raised from seed one year and produces its flowers during the following one.*

BULB: *An underground food storage organ formed of fleshy, modified leaves that enclose a dormant shoot.*

BULBIL: *A small, immature bulb that grows around the base of a mature bulb. It can be removed and encouraged to grow.*

CALCAREOUS: *Growing in chalky or limy soil.*

CALCIFUGE: *A plant that hates lime and therefore needs soil that is neutral or acid.*

CLOCHE: *Originally a bell-shaped cover used to protect plants. Now, it means a wide range of low glass or plastic-covered structures.*

COMPOST: *Has a dual meaning. Refers to the mixture in which cuttings are inserted, seeds sown and plants repotted. It can also be used to describe decomposed vegetable waste.*

CORM: *A swollen and thickened stem base covered with a papery skin. At a corm's top there is a shoot which produces a further shoot as well as roots.*

CULTIVARS: *A variety which has been raised in cultivation, rather than appearing naturally without any interference from man.*

DEAD-HEADING: *The removal of faded flower heads to prevent the formation of seeds and to encourage the development of further flowers.*

DECIDUOUS: *A plant that sheds all of its leaves in autumn and produces a fresh array of them in spring. Such plants usually have a woody and permanent nature, such as trees and shrubs. Some conifers are deciduous, but most are evergreen.*

DORMANT: *The period – usually in winter – when a plant is resting.*

DRY-STONE WALL: *Walls formed of natural stone and without the benefit of mortar to hold them together. Some dry-stone walls are used to retain soil and to form different levels, while others can be free-standing, forming a wall in which plants can be grown.*

DWARF CONIFERS: *Conifers that remain small throughout their life.*

ERICACEOUS: *Plants belonging to the Ericaceae family and including heathers and heaths.*

EVERGREEN: *Shrubs, trees and conifers that appear to be green throughout the year and not to lose their leaves. In reality, however, they shed some of their leaves throughout the year, while producing others.*

FARINA: *Literally means a dusting with a white powder. Some plants, such as certain primulas, have leaves coated in this way.*

FRIABLE: *Soil that is crumbly and light and easily worked. It especially applies to soil being prepared as a seed-bed in spring.*

FUNGICIDE: *A chemical for controlling or eliminating fungal diseases. Some fungicides are systemic and enter a plant's sap-stream.*

GARDEN COMPOST: *Vegetable waste from kitchens and soft parts of garden plants which are encouraged to decompose and to form a material that can be dug into soil or used to create a mulch around plants.*

GLAUCOUS: *Blue or grey-green, and usually used to describe leaves and stems.*

HALF-HARDY: *Plants that are not sufficiently hardy to withstand the rigours of cold and wet winters in temperate climates. Many plants from warm countries cannot survive cold winters, but are well able to thrive there during summer.*

HALF-HARDY ANNUALS: *Tender annuals, raised in gentle warmth in late winter or early spring, slowly acclimatized to outdoor conditions and planted outside in borders, containers and rock gardens as soon as all risk of frost has passed.*

HARDY: *A plant that is able to survive outdoors in winter. In the case of some rock-garden plants good drainage is essential to their survival.*

HYBRID: *A plant resulting from a cross between two distinct species or genera. These plants usually reveal great vigour and uniformity.*

MULCHING: *Covering the soil around plants with well-decayed organic material such as garden compost, peat or, in the case of rock garden plants, stone chippings or 6mm/1¼in of shingle.*

LOAM: *Friable topsoil. It should not be predominantly clay, neither can it be of a sandy nature.*

NEUTRAL: *Soil that is neither acid nor alkaline, with a pH of 7.0. However, most plants thrive in a pH of about 6.5.*

PEAT BED: *Areas where acid-loving plants can be grown. They are formed of compressed peat blocks instead of rocks, with the soil mainly of peat. Logs and old wooden railway sleepers can be used to constrain the soil.*

PERENNIAL: *A plant that persists from one year to another. Some have an herbaceous nature, with the stems and leaves dying down to soil-level in winter; others reveal a woody framework, such as trees and shrubs.*

pH: *A measure of the acidity or alkalinity of soil, assessed on a logarithmic scale which ranges from 0 to 14, with 7.0 as the chemical neutral figure.*

POTTING COMPOST: *Compost formed of loam, sharp sand and peat. The ratio of these main ingredients is altered according to whether the compost is used for sowing seeds, potting-up or repotting plants into larger containers.*

RAISED BED: *A raised area encircled by a dry-stone wall. Rock-garden plants can be grown both in the raised bed and the wall. These beds can usually be reached by people who garden from wheelchairs.*

SCREE BED: *An area formed of small stones and rocks, usually at the base of a rock garden.*

SINK GARDENS: *Old stone sinks when partly filled with drainage material and then with freely-draining compost can be planted with small rock-garden plants. These features are ideal for positioning on patios.*

SLOW-GROWING CONIFERS: *Conifers that grow slowly and therefore when young can be planted in a rock garden. Later, when too large, they are usually moved into a garden.*

STRATA: *The natural layers of rocks. This is frequently simulated when building a rock garden.*

SUB-SHRUB: *Small and spreading shrub, with a woody base. It differs from normal shrubs in that when grown in temperate regions its upper stems and shoots die back each winter.*

TILTH: *Friable topsoil, in which seeds can be sown. It also acts as a mulch on the surface of soil, helping to reduce the loss of moisture from soil.*

TUFA: *A type of rock, with a porous nature. Plants can be grown in it.*

VARIEGATED: *Usually applied to leaves and used to describe a state of having two or more colours.*

VARIETY: *A natural occurring variation within a species of plant.*

INDEX